About the Author

I have had more jobs than I can count, travelled to dozens of different countries. Taken on problems that I thought I would not be able to manage, but with the help of my higher self, as I call it, nothing is too big for anyone. We come here with nothing and leave with something, wisdom. These days I reside in Tasmania where the air is clean and the natural energy is abundant, this natural energy is food for the soul, it's as essential as a good breakfast is for the body. Take life head on, we all underestimate ourselves.

Trust

Geoff Parton

Trust

Olympia Publishers
London

www.olympiapublishers.com
OLYMPIA PAPERBACK EDITION

Copyright © Geoff Parton 2023

The right of Geoff Parton to be identified as author of
this work has been asserted in accordance with sections 77 and 78 of
the Copyright, Designs and Patents Act 1988.

All Rights Reserved

No reproduction, copy or transmission of this publication
may be made without written permission.
No paragraph of this publication may be reproduced,
copied or transmitted save with the written permission of the publisher,
or in accordance with the provisions
of the Copyright Act 1956 (as amended).

Any person who commits any unauthorised act in relation to
this publication may be liable to criminal
prosecution and civil claims for damage.

A CIP catalogue record for this title is
available from the British Library.

ISBN: 978-1-80074-611-4

First Published in 2023

Olympia Publishers
Tallis House
2 Tallis Street
London
EC4Y 0AB

Printed in Great Britain

Dedication

To my wife, Jayne, for putting up with me, and to all those that seek spiritual advancement.

Chapter 1

The Early Days

I was born in 1948, at that time my family lived on a chicken farm in an area known as Duffy's Forest in New South Wales, Australia. In those days, Duffy's Forest was mostly untouched bush with a few houses scattered here and there. It bordered Ku-ring-gai Chase, a name taken from the Guringai aboriginal people. The chase is a large area of almost fifteen thousand hectares of bushland. Today it is National Park, but in those days, it was just natural bush for anybody to explore. The park runs from Terry Hills right up to Berowra and Hornsby. Meandering right through the middle of it is Cowan creek, a beautiful tributary of the Hawkesbury River. On this tributary lies the picturesque tiny hamlet of Bobbin Head, which is home to a small marina and has barely changed since I was a child.

Living on a farm that bordered this enormous bush land — was fantastic; somehow it seemed as though it all belonged to me!

Our farm was ten acres in size and had two small dams and a pretty little creek running right through the centre of the property. About a third of the property was still natural bush land, so there was still plenty of room for a young boy to get into mischief.

My father always looked the same; he always wore long grey trousers and a blue chequered fleecy shirt with sleeves partly rolled up. He never wore a hat, rarely wore shorts, and always wore boots as there was plenty of snakes around!

He was a chicken farmer — he built several large sheds where young chickens ran free. There were also numerous small sheds which housed the more adult fouls. They were also able to run free during the day, but at night they had to be caged up again otherwise feral cats or foxes would eat them. Outside from the farm, there were many tracks leading through the Ku-ring-Gai Chase; they were mostly fire trails which gave access to fire trucks when a bush fire was imminent, which seemed to happen every couple of years. I remember quite well being young boy and the bushfire was no more than ten metres away from the house. My brother, sister and mother, also my father, all had 'knapsack 'sprayers on our backs, they were a bit like a backpack with a handheld pump. It was a bit like trying to put a bushfire out with a bucket! But that's all we had. One time, Mum put a big blanket out in the middle of the grassy field and took out some personal belongings that she valued. I didn't realise at the time but, she and my father thought that they were going to lose the house.

In the chase, I was always exploring the old fire tracks whenever I had a free moment. Smaller animal tracks mostly belonging to kangaroo and other creatures, were more enticing and interesting for me. Over the years, I discovered quite a number of aboriginal rock carvings. I would often camp near them because they fascinated me. I sometimes slept out under the stars at night, I would just lie there looking at the stars and wondering what life must've been like living as an aboriginal. I often wished, that somehow, I could be with them and part of them, away from the farm life which for me was mostly unhappy.

While exploring these sites, I found old burned-out fires left from centuries before. With some charcoal from the fires in hand, I would trace the outline of the rock carvings so that I could see them more clearly, I was then able to get a better picture of the messages they had been left for me. Aboriginal rock carvings almost always have a message — for others.

For example, a row of fish carved into the rock usually meant that following the direction that the row was pointing, you would find they led directly to a good fishing hole on the river. There were many other examples, some depicting the type of animals or game that were plentiful in the area. Even today not many people know the whereabouts of those rock carvings I found.

In those days I felt I was a bit like an explorer, as nobody else had penetrated deep into these areas for well over a hundred years, it was fascinating for me.

When a person goes to an area that has not had humans in it for a very long time, there is a strong natural feeling — like it has started to revert back to its natural clean state. By clean state I mean unpolluted by artificial energy — coming mostly from humans. It becomes fresh with new natural energy from the flora, fauna, and the spirit world; you can sense it and feel it — people who penetrate into native bushland, get a lovely sense of peace immediately with nature. It's very important for us all to have time with nature, as it's part of our spiritual diet. Most people crave this energy unknowingly.

Just stop and think about it, what do people do when they want to get away? They leave their nice houses with all the trimmings and go camping! Even those that have nice caravans mostly tend to sit outside in the elements on some uncomfortable canvas chair by a small fire. Why? Because we long for this natural energy and to be close to nature. It's absolutely essential for the spirit.

A six hour walk from the farm to Cowan Creek would take me to a place called Duffy's Wharf, constructed by Peter Duffy in the mid-1850s for the timber industry. The walk from the farm was almost all downhill through thick lush bushland, following a narrow winding track that also seemed to follow a small meandering creek. The track to Duffy's Wharf was long and difficult, it was no more than a wallaby track. The walk usually meant a night had to be spent before the challenging return walk back up the steep mountain.

I would leave early in the morning, at that time the track was often wet with either dew or rain. Ferns that lined the track would glisten as the early sunlight struggled to penetrate the tall trees. Moss grew on almost every log that I had to clamber over, so by the time I reached Duffy's Wharf it was usually time for a refreshing swim to wash off.

In those days Duffy's Wharf was no more than a broken-down sign that read 'ring bell for ferry'…. The bell was missing even when I was just an eight-year-old kid. The ferry had operated sometime in the mid to late-1800s. It was a beautiful spot, there were remnants of a burnt-out hull — possibly the ferry that lay almost fully submerged with only part of the bow exposed to the weather. Other than the wreck and the sign, there were no indications that any humans other than myself had ever been there.

This was part of Cowan Creek, at this particular point the creek was approximately sixty metres wide and was already almost salt water… back up the river it became more brackish.

In the shallow waters, small stingrays could be seen trying to hide at the sound of my approach flapping their wings as they buried themselves in the sand. There was a shallow cave nearby where I would sleep, it was deep enough to keep me dry from unexpected rain or heavy dew.

At night I would light a small fire to keep away anything that might be lurking nearby, small creatures like possums, bandicoots and bush rats would make their presence known all through the night, as they tried hard to steal any food scraps that I may have left around. Occasionally I would take a friend from school with me, they often found it quite frightening but I was used to the noises and it didn't bother me a bit.

My father had told me stories about the Chinese back in the 1800s. He said they had a 'still' hidden somewhere in the bush, where they would make and bottle alcohol illegally — relabelling it which they would then transport it by river to Sydney to be sold as imported alcohol on the black market.

No matter how hard I searched, I never found the still! Although there were remnants of old bullock tracks, I had found from time to time. It was a romantic story, I continued to look for evidence to support this story.

Living on a farm in Australia in the late-1940s' and early-50's, there was virtually no communication, we didn't even have electricity or the phone on. Television was unheard of then but we did have a radio. The radio was one of those great big wooden ones that stood about three feet high and was powered from an old truck battery. The radio was everything — it was the focal point in our living room and meant contact with the outside world. At night time we would sit and listen to our favourite radio shows; they were serialised and were mostly westerns of some sort.

Most of the stories had horses in them, I remember hearing the clip clop, clip clop of hooves, the jingle of the bridles and men saying, "Whoa" to their horses to stop. I felt I was there... I could almost smell the horses and dust, it was fantastic. I think it's where I got my yearning to have a horse!

Not having television meant that we used our imagination. You see watching television inhibits the use of your imagination unlike having a story read to you or listening to the radio, where your imagination is let loose to go anywhere!

At night after dinner, my sister and I would wash the dishes and sing together. When we had finished, the radio was turned on and we would listen to our favourite shows letting our imaginations run away. We used to listen to shows like 'Search for the Golden Boomerang' (my favourite), or 'Dad & Dave' and other great stories of that time. Looking back, I realise how much better the radio was than a TV, because children and adults alike could imagine the story in their mind, and there's really no telling where that ends up.

Because I was free to use my imagination, I became open to all possibilities unlike kids of today who are dominated by computers and plugs-ins of all kinds. One only has to try to communicate with young ones today, it soon becomes hard to work out whether they are listening to you or something else that's going through the wires attached to their ears!

I'm not running the kids of today down, but I feel saddened when I see the amount of time that is spent on artificial things like computer games, television, and my pet hate — texting. They are texting, texting, instead of talking, talking, talking. You name it, all these things are artificial and block access to natural and spiritual learning.

In saying that, these gadgets are wonderful in many ways, but it is very easy to become addicted to them. I'm very glad that I was brought up in the 1950s when those things didn't exist.

I left primary school when I was twelve years old, and

completed only seven months of the first year in high school. I was then put to work full time on the farm. I always thought that not having much of an education had been a handicap as it prevented me from getting 'good' jobs throughout my life. Later on, I realised, that the lack of conventional education turned out to be my greatest asset as it helped to open my 'special door.' I was so glad I didn't turn out like a processed pea unable to think for myself. The special door I'm referring to is my connection with the spiritual world.

Our lives today seem to be so pre-organised by governments, schools and sports, like football, cricket, tennis, or golf. Practically every waking moment of your life is occupied leaving absolutely no time for self-development. We call this natural, but I doubt this… it has become normal — but it's not natural.

The house that my father built had a thick corrugated fibro roof and a hardwood frame. It was lined both inside and out with fibro sheeting. My father designed and built the house completely on his own with no plans — just a drawing from his head, and also without the use of any electrical tools as we had no electricity! It still stands today. My father had a limited amount of hand tools; just a hammer, two or three different grades of hand saws, and a good selection of spanners.

Having a hard wood frame meant nails were very difficult to hammer in. I can remember cakes of yellow sunlight soap scattered about the building site with holes all through them like they had been shot at with a shot gun; but these holes were where my father would force a nail into the soap in order to make it slippery, it would then be easier to penetrate the hardwood when being hit with the hammer.

All building materials had to be purchased from Sydney which was a long way away. We didn't have a car, just an old

Essex truck which was already about thirty years old at the time. I remember it well, it was green and had a sort of soft top on the cabin and timbered, spoked wheels. It used to whine and scream and seemed to take forever to get anywhere. There was nothing easy about life on the farm, the house was never finished! Mum was sometimes heard grumbling about that, plus the fact that it was also never painted. Looking back, I don't think the house ever got painted or finished totally.

The house was very basic, it consisted of a dining room, a kitchen, one main bedroom, a bathroom and the lounge room. A U-shaped veranda partially surrounded the house, the section where we slept was enclosed with hessian blinds. There were three beds on the veranda, one for each of us kids. My brother had the biggest one, and my sister and I had the other two smaller ones. The blankets were dark grey, World War II surplus. The hessian blinds were rolled down for winter and up for summer, they were the only protection from the weather.

The other part of the veranda was used for mixing chicken feed. There my father had an old bath where he would mix all the ingredients together, to make it. I can remember dried powdered milk in big lumps which had to be rolled and crushed finely enough to go through a sieve before numerous other ingredients were added, to obtain the best balance for the fowl's diet.

The small lounge room had an open fire that was only lit when it was extremely cold. The only other heating we had was a kerosene heater, and of course the slow combustion wood stove. I remember in the middle of winter, sometimes I would go outside and find the water in the chicken's water troughs had frozen. It got pretty cold, and most of the time I still went without shoes!

Although the house was never completely painted, the

kitchen was eventually done in the early-60s. It was painted in very 1960s colours, pink cupboard doors with black plastic knobs on them. It all looked very modern then. The back door, which somehow always seemed to be used as the front door, had an enormous lemon tree growing no more than ten yards away. Alongside that was a very large mulberry tree. There was a small garden around the base of the lemon tree where Mum would grow parsley, mint and other herbs. At the side of the garden was a post with a butter churner attached to it... At the corner of the house there was an old square rusty water tank that collected rainwater from the house roof for drinking. Close by there was an out-house which was also part of the small woodshed.

Having our daily wash meant boiling water during the day on the old Metter's slow combustion wood stove. Mum cooked all the meals on it, so once it was lit in the mornings, it would be kept going all day, summer and winter.

After washing in a tub for years, we eventually got a hot water service for the bathroom which ran on kerosene. However, taking a shower was still quite an undertaking... The new hot water unit had to be lit — then pumped to create pressure turning the liquid kerosene into a gas, a very hot blue flame would then be produced to heat the water successfully. A very close eye had to be kept on it otherwise the pressure would drop, making the kerosene re-liquefy again, causing it to burn very black. If that happened, it would send the whole bathroom black with soot! This happened on a number of occasions leaving a major job to clean the bathroom and everything in it — the walls, the mirror, the heater, and the bath. Somehow, we seemed to get almost as much on each other as we got off the walls! After cleaning for several hours, we would come out blacker than a chimney sweep. The other thing that had to be constantly watched was the water flow. The water had to be kept running otherwise the water would get too hot for the unit and boil, risking an explosion. Fortunately, that never happened. The hot water unit itself was totally nickel plated, it had beautiful scrollwork on it probably dating from the turn of the century. Today it would certainly be a collector's item. Strangely enough it had been appropriately named by its makers the 'Challenge Hot Water Heater.'

It was a great event when we got our first refrigerator, like most things in those days it ran on kerosene, it was called a Silent Night. By today's standards it was small and inefficient, but in those days, it was fantastic after not having a fridge at all. Fresh milk from our cow was placed on a deep tray on the bottom shelf of the fridge overnight. As the milk cooled down, the cream would separate and rise, it could then be skimmed off the following morning. A small amount of the cream was kept for father's breakfast, the rest was taken out to the butter churner mounted on the post outside the kitchen window. There my sister and I would take turns winding the thing around and around for hours — until the cream would slowly turn into butter, it was an arm aching job. The butter would then be taken into the kitchen where Mum would shape it with little flat wooden butter patties. Sometimes she would curl the butter or simply leave it in an oblong shape.

My mother didn't drive in those days, my father had the old green Essex truck that was built sometime in 1924. It was often difficult to start, and when it did go it went very slowly. My father used the truck to take fowls in cages to the open market in Sydney where they were sold. Sydney was about twenty miles away from the farm, it doesn't sound far now, but in an old Essex truck that had a top speed of about thirty-five miles an hour, coupled with the shocking roads, it took us about two hours just to get there.

On the return trip mail would be picked up from the post office, that was usually once or twice a week if we were lucky. The groceries had to be ordered with Mum's handwritten list. They would be delivered to the farm a few days later... as it was a weekly service if you forgot something you went without it! Wood had to be cut and the cow had to be milked to make butter. Eggs had to be collected for breakfast, and vegetables were grown in the garden. It was a lot of work just to exist. Mum had to boil water in an old copper for all the washing. She lit a fire burning underneath it to heat the water, then it would have to be rinsed and hung up on the line to dry — there was no washing machine. The ironing was also a major task as the iron had to be heated on the stove as well.

We had two cows, one of which gave milk. Her name was Patsy, she was light brown in colour, she had huge open welcoming eyes with great big eyelashes, and she was just beautiful. Mum or my brother would milk her, there was another cow called Patches, she was also light brown with great big white patches, hence her name. She may have been Patsy's daughter as I remember a big cow trying to play leapfrog with Patsy the year before.

"NOURISH THE SPIRIT."

Chapter 2

School Days

It was about four and a half miles to school on a gravel road which was rough and pot-holed. The bus was an old slow vehicle that was completely devoid of any style, so much so that the kids nicknamed it the 'Butter Box' — as it seemed to be totally square.

After paying the three-penny bus fare, it became a scramble to get to the back seat before any of the other kids did, because the back seat was the place to be. When the bus started to move down the road, it would lurch as it crawled away, making grinding noises from somewhere underneath. It seemed to take hours to get to school, I remember looking out of the window and saying to myself, 'I could run faster than this!'

The bus stop was about one and a half miles away from the farm — so that meant a walk. Sometimes we would ride our bikes to the bus stop and hide them in the bush until the afternoon — then we would race each other back to the farm. Sometimes I rode my bike to school, it was usually just as fast as the bus anyway even though the bikes were old and second-hand, like everything else we had.

The saved bus fare would go towards a treat from the local grocery store the following afternoon — that's if Mum didn't remember or didn't realise that I had ridden my bike. We didn't have a lot of money in those days, I often used string for my shoelaces, but that didn't matter because most of the time I took my shoes off anyway and hid them in the bush so I could go to school barefoot.

The school was tiny with one big room where all classes were attended, right up to twelfth class. In the mornings, after the second bell rang, we all had to line up then march into the room. Lining up meant someone had to be at the front of the line. It seemed there was always a battle between me and another boy to see who got there first. I wouldn't say I was aggressive, in fact I was very shy, but I always seemed to be getting into a fight with someone. A torn shirt, a bit of skin off the knees or anywhere else, didn't seem to matter to me. The only time it really mattered was when I broke my glasses which happened a number of times. When it did happen, I got into a lot of trouble from my father… It always meant a hiding from him.

On one occasion when my brother and I were on the farm, we were having one of many arguments. He hit me and knocked my glasses off my face, I was just six at the time and we couldn't find them anywhere, he was terrified he would be in trouble thinking I would tell on him. It was almost dark so he said, "Let's light a little fire so we can search for them by the firelight." That made some sense, so we lit a small fire and went on searching, after searching for several hours we eventually had to go back to the house. Both sitting at the dinner table, we were hoping that Mum or Dad wouldn't notice that I wasn't wearing my glasses, but inevitably Mum asked, "Where are your glasses?" Confident of finding them the next morning, we'd made up a story that I'd left them on the top of a fence post in the paddock. My brother kept looking at me wondering if I would tell on him but I didn't. We got away with that and the next morning, both of us ran up to where we had lit the fire to look for my glasses. Well, we found them all right, they were right in the middle of the grey ashes of the small fire from the night before! All that was left was a piece of bent wire from the frames and a couple of dirty cracked lenses. When we got back to the house later, we both got it from my father!

At the school, construction work had started on an additional building eventually adding to our one room school, which meant a new teacher. Up until then, I had only ever had a male teacher who was also the principal or the headmaster, as we called them in those days. To my delight the new teacher was a lady. I was immediately smitten with Mrs Whoolmer. It was just great to have a female teacher because somehow, she didn't seem as tough so I wasn't scared of her. School was a place I hated, but I was always glad to get there as it meant getting away from my father, and the constant trouble I seemed to be in always.

One day, when I was about seven years old, we were told by the teacher that the following week we were going to see a movie at the school. The next week seemed to drag out as we waited for the big day to come round. At that time, I had never seen a movie, I remember it like it was yesterday. The teachers came in and darkened the main room… We all sat and waited, then we heard the click, click, click, click of the projector, and on the big white screen that was now hanging over the blackboard, came some writing and with-it music was heard.

The movie was called 'Little Women', it was in black and white… It was the biggest eye opener for me — I couldn't believe that right in front of me on the wall, were three beautiful girls dressed in clothes of a type I had never seen before. They spoke with an accent, I had never heard anybody speak so differently to the way we spoke, I was dumbfounded, it was just incredible! I just wanted to get up and climb into the movie somehow to be there with them, escape, escape!

For once all the kids in the class were quiet much to the teachers' delight, as we all just sat there gazing at the movie. For the first time in my life, I realised that there was something else other than the chicken farm out there! I'm sure now that it was a catalyst for me, I realised then and there, that there was another life waiting for me.

About a mile away from the school was a grocery shop, it was the only shop around other than the post office. Occasionally the shopkeeper would sell me a penny's worth of broken biscuits from the bus fare I had saved.

In those days biscuits were delivered to shops in big bulk tins, then they were weighed on scales, and placed in brown paper bags — then re-sold to the customer... As a result, there was always some broken biscuits left in the bottom of the big tins, which were unsaleable. The shopkeeper saved them up for us kids to buy after school, and that was a real treat as I was always hungry...

My father always said I had hollow legs.

The post office was nearby and was one of the smallest shops in the country! There was room for just one person to stand behind a small counter, the whole building was about twice the size our outhouse (meaning the outside 'dunny' or toilet).

On the odd occasion when I went into the post office, I found that it always had that smell of print, glue, and general oldness. I was never sure whether the smell was from the stamps or from the old woman who ran the post office! She had grey hair with virtually no style to it and was always dressed in drab clothes. When I would go into the post office, she always seemed to have an accusing look on her face, it made me feel like I'd done something wrong... I didn't like her!

"THE CATALYST"

Chapter 3

Schmoon Valley

In around 1953 we got the phone on, what a breakthrough that was! We were the first people in the district to get a phone and the word spread quickly. As a result, we often had the neighbours knocking at the door wanting to use it. It was a wooden box thing that was attached to the wall. It had a handle on the side that Mum would have to wind madly, then she would wait until a distant voice was heard. It seemed like magic to me… There was an earpiece that was attached by a cable to the box, and on the box, there was a mouthpiece that you spoke into, it was just amazing. I used to sit by the phone trying to figure out how Mum could speak to somebody who wasn't in the house and couldn't be seen!

A few miles away from the farm, there lived a group of people, Mum considered them to be 'unusual', as they lived together in a type of commune in the bush, in a place they called Schmoon Valley… There were probably about fifteen of them. Having the phone on had made us very popular, because we often received messages for other people — as well as our neighbours. Because my brother was the oldest, he was often sent out either on foot or push bike to deliver such messages. One day when my brother was about twelve, he was asked to take a message to the leader of the Schmoon Valley group. When he returned, Mum asked him, "Did you give Mr. Wilson the message?" When he nodded, Mum asked what the man had been doing… My brother said with much emphasis, "He was chopping wood and all he had on was a hanky tied around his head!" I think Mum soon realised the group was a nudist colony, hence Schmoon Valley became off-limits and we were never allowed to go down there again.

"PEOPLE GETTING BACK TO NATURE."

Chapter 4

A Strange Lunch

At home when I was allowed to play, it was always outside by the creek. Every winter on the farm the creek would flood. Sometimes my father would have to drive the tractor through it pulling a load of chicken feed or something else on the trailer. I just loved to see the creek flooded and the water rushing along.

The creek meandered down through the property where two dams were built for water storage. It would then pass underneath the road through storm water pipes and continue down, cascading over a series of beautiful waterfalls which then formed small rock pools. I would often play in the rock pools, which were mostly about the size of a large bathtub, one or two being much larger. They had numerous little crevices and holes created by the flowing water over hundreds of years, it was a magical place. Sometimes I would climb carefully down the side of the bank to the largest waterfall, there I would take a shower under the flowing water. In behind the waterfall was a large cave that always seemed mysterious. Climbing in behind the waterfall seemed very private and secluded. There was a feeling that time didn't exist there, because nothing seemed to have ever changed. It was just an amazing place — like a fairyland really with the sun glistening through the water as it fell to the rocky pool below. I loved it, it was my favourite part of the farm.

The rain seemed to bring out lots of yabbies from where they were hiding in their holes on the muddy banks of the creek. I would spend hours playing by the creek trying to catch them. If you want to catch one the trick is to attach a small portion of meat on a piece of string, then dangle it in front of one of the holes in the creek bank to entice the yabby out! If you're lucky, you'll see some movement and a big nipper will come out and try and take the meat off the string... one has to be very still and watch carefully. Once the yabby feels he is no longer in danger, he will try to pull the meat off the string. When he is engrossed in this task, it's fairly easy to slowly pull the string up. When the yabby is just under the water, a quick jerk of the string can often land the yabby on the bank, where you have to take care not to have your finger nipped, he can then be easily be placed in a bucket. They are simple to cook to make a nice meal.

My father had told me that when he was a young boy, he used to have tadpoles on toast! Apparently, this turned out to be a joke, but one day when Mum and Dad were out, my sister and I were left alone... I was probably about six years old, so my sister would have been about ten. She was in charge, and when lunchtime came, I can't remember who suggested it, but after hearing my father's story so often, we thought we'd have tadpoles on toast. We took an empty jar from Mum's cupboard and went down to the creek. There were hundreds of tadpoles so it was only a matter of choosing the fattest — we proceeded to fill the jar! It wasn't long before we had the jar of tadpoles back in the kitchen. Not knowing how to cook them, we decided to slightly boil them but not too much as they were tender and might fall to pieces. I remember they changed colour from their original black to a pale blue grey colour. We didn't know which part to eat the tail, the head, or both, but I didn't want to eat their little eyes so I thought, that at least the eyes should be cut off. That meant cutting off about half their head, we didn't want to take too much off as there would be nothing left to eat! We made two slices of toast and buttered them, then we carefully placed the grey slimy tadpoles on the toast. We added pepper and salt and then proceeded to devour them. That afternoon when Mum and Dad came home, Mum asked, "Have you been good children?" We replied in the affirmative, she then asked, "What did you have for lunch?" When we said we had tadpoles on toast, Mum just looked at us while my father exploded with laughter. I guess I knew then that we were the victims of a joke.

"TRICKERY."

Chapter 5

The Snake

Late for the school bus as usual, I was running down the small track on the farm which passed by the two dams... it was a shortcut to catch the waiting school bus. The track was slippery and with many rocks, but I was very nimble and rarely if ever fell over.

This particular morning it was warm and sunny. Halfway between the first dam and the second one there was a log lying across the track, it had been there for many years I always jumped over it and ran on. The track went on for another hundred metres or so before finally coming out of the bush — then, entering the dirt road, I would continue my sprint to the waiting bus.

This particular morning, I ran past the first dam and onto the second dam. Approaching the log, I jumped as I had done dozens of times before, but this time when I was in the air, I saw a large black snake lying on the ground right where I was to have landed! I knew in an instant that if I landed on top of the snake I would have been bitten, but while I was in the air, I felt an invisible power carrying me further and further away from the snake. When I did land, it was at least eight feet further beyond the log — well out of striking distance! The only explanation, it was a divine power from a higher source that propelled me an extra eight feet, therefore saving my life that day!

My father had always told me when walking in the bush to

look down, not ahead, I was glad that I had listened. That afternoon, I couldn't wait to get home and tell the family at the dinner table what had happened that morning with the snake and the long jump. As usual I was ridiculed; they told me I was stupid and it was simply impossible — but I knew what had happened, as on a number of other occasions similar things happened.

I had a close school friend who had a beautiful sister whom I had a crush on. We were both twelve years old. Erica was her name; I was absolutely besotted with her. When her family moved into the area, she started to catch the school bus. I was very shy, and looking back I think she probably knew how I felt as I couldn't stop staring at her. On the way home from school on the bus each afternoon, I would just sit there looking at her, I always sat a couple of seats back from her. I decided to write little notes on small pieces of paper telling her of my innermost feelings that I felt for her. When she alighted from the bus, I would watch her walking away, I would throw my little messages out of the bus window somehow believing that she would return and retrieve them. I would continue on the bus until the next stop which was the last stop. The bus terminated there before setting off on the return journey.

I would walk back to the farm unable to get her out of my mind, after my chores were done, I would contemplate on what a stupid thing I had done — leaving the messages at the bus stop. I'd run back to the bus stop in a panic, hoping that none of the other kids found my love notes. Sometimes when I could sneak away in the late afternoon, I would go up to my friend's house which was about two kilometres away to play, to get another look at his beautiful sister Erica. I would take the shortest route I knew through the bush. The track I took hadn't been used for years, and it was washed out with numerous pot holes unsuitable for any vehicle to use. When it came close to dark, I would head off home running. I loved running — I ran everywhere... it seemed I had endless amounts of energy, I also knew I had to get home quickly for fear I would be in trouble if I was late. I had one thing in my favour, the track was mostly downhill, I would run like the wind trying to straddle the big pot-holes... I would start to take great leaps to avoid them. These leaps, with the help of my invisible friend, became enormous, over several meters at a time. I thought this was quite normal, but I realised later in life it was not possible for a young boy of twelve to do — unless he had help like me. My invisible friend who saved me from the snake was always with me enabling me to do things that I now realise were not normal.

It was almost like flying, it continued to happen many times. I felt extremely light as though there was not much gravity holding me down, I felt supported by this mysterious power. While it may seem strange to others, it seemed quite natural to me. I loved the sensation of being able to take these giant leaps, although it was not something I could or did talk about to others, it remained my secret until now.

Many years later, I had another helping hand from my 'spirit'. I had been camping with my daughter who was about five years old at the time. It was a beautiful day so we went swimming, she, as a five-year-old, was now taking a nap in our tent which was close by. I was taking time out sitting on the edge of a rock pool with my legs dangling over the ice-cold swimming hole. The swimming hole was fed by a storm water pipe running under a causeway. A small amount of water was running over the causeway, but the majority was pouring through the storm water pipe ending up in the small pond where I was sitting, before cascading down a rocky waterfall several hundred feet below.

On the other side of the causeway there were other children swimming. While some water was running over the causeway the water in general looked very calm and tranquil, but there was the storm water pipe! Just looking at the surface of the water it was hard to get any indication that just under the surface, there was a massive amount of water being sucked through the storm pipe.

A young girl about eleven years old was swimming there, she didn't realise there was a storm water pipe sucking masses of water through it, down to the pool on the other side of the causeway. Swimming and not paying attention, she got too close to the suction of the pipe and was immediately pulled through under the concrete causeway, where I was sitting on the other side. In an instant she was through the pipe half drowning. — I was the only person there, so in a split second without a thought, I jumped into the pool fully clothed! My eyes opened to see the young girl sideways floating and clearly shocked, she was making no attempt to get to the surface, probable she had lost all direction. Suddenly I found I had super strength! I picked her out of the water like she was a rag doll and placed her onto a rock, where for a moment she struggled to get her breath. Moments later she recovered and then started to cry, I spoke to her to calm her down. How she had not hit her head when she was sucked under the causeway is beyond me.

She soon regained her composure, then without warning she got up and ran back to her family who at that time had no idea what had just happened. The point that I am making here, is that a helping hand from above had given me the strength to rescue her without any thought or concern for the ice-cold water… I just responded.

I have heard of other people doing similar things, when they get told they are heroes they just say, "I did it without thinking really." This is the power of the spirit, it's able to control the body and make it jump into ice cold water fully clothed without thinking or even feeling the temperature. It can also give one the extra strength if needed (it was effortless by the way) just as I was able to jump well clear of the snake and take giant long jumps — just for fun when I was a young boy.

If you trust, pretty much anything is possible. We are **not** limited by our physical bodies — at a pinch, the spirit can and does sometimes take over completely.

"THE POWER IS THERE, USE IT."

Chapter 6

Liquorice

In the early days on the farm, I had no one my age to play with, my older brother was in high school, and my sister was also at school, as a result I used to play by myself down by the creek. Many times, I found a 'little friend' there — at the age of six I thought it was quite natural! He just seemed to appear and be with me. He was black skinned and about my size. I always thought he was Indian or something like that, although I had never seen an Indian. As a result, I named him Liquorice, because that was the only thing I could think of, that was about the same colour as he was.

My hide away by the creek where I used to go was very secluded, thanks to the reeds and twisted branches that kept it well hidden. It had a beautiful small waterfall, just water running over a few rocks really, but to me at that age it seemed larger.

Liquorice became my best friend and only friend, he was always there for me. He usually sat opposite me, we would talk and talk, he was as real to me as if he was my brother. Mum asked me one day, "What have you been doing?" I answered, "I've been playing with Liquorice." I remember her asking me where I got the liquorice from as she must have thought it was something I was eating, so I told her, "He is my friend."

"Hmmm she said with a smile, "Does he have a second name?"

"Yes," I said, "All sorts."

One day she asked me, "Why do you call him Liquorice?" I told her, "Because he's black." At that age I had never seen a black person other than Liquorice. I was very surprised from the look on Mum's face when she repeated the word, "BLACK." He was the only friend I had for a long, long time.

One day we were in Sydney in a big department store, we didn't get to Sydney very often as it meant a long bus ride and a big day out. Going to the city for me was overwhelming, people everywhere but the best thing I liked about it was the lifts. In the big department stores, there were lifts up and down to the different levels, there was a man driving the lift, he had a little tool he used to open and shut the doors, one of which was a sliding security door, he would then announce what was on the next level so everybody in the lift new that the next level might be menswear, or perhaps ladies wear. I would watch in fascination as he shut the door and then turned the handle and the lift would move either up or down, fascinating for a kid from the bush.

On one occasion in the lift, I heard somebody say something about eating Liquorice all-sorts. I immediately responded by yelling out, "BUT HE'S A KID!" My mum was quite embarrassed at my outburst. Eventually somebody, either my brother or my father told me Liquorice was "not real," and I was stupid with an incredible imagination. That got me thinking, and of course the logical left brain took control of my thinking. So I started to think, 'Maybe he's not real.' From that moment on when I went down to play by the creek, I found that Liquorice was not there every time. Our meetings became more and more infrequent. He eventually disappeared out of my life, I missed him greatly but I never saw him again.

Some people call this childhood imagination, but I know otherwise. You see the reason that it's mostly children who see these so-called imaginary people, is because they are open-minded and use their right brain more than there left brain. The left brain is the logical thinking brain, the right brain is where we get all our messages from above, if you like. These messages we receive often don't make much sense, and so we revert back to using our left brain the logic, but as soon as this happens, we lose our opportunity with our connection with our higher self, or spiritual world, whatever you like to call it. Adults are, as we all are, trained to use the logical left brain only. When I became convinced Liquorice didn't exist, then he ceased to exist!

"STAY OPEN MINDED."

Chapter 7

Pig Tails

On the farm one Saturday, my sister went to Chatswood on the bus which was about fourteen miles away. The trip took almost an hour — for a young girl of eleven years old it was a big deal to be allowed out on her own. At that time the bus terminated about a mile and half away from the farm, it meant a long walk both ways. Mum asked me to get on my bike and go and meet my sister at the bus stop. I was about eight years old.

I arrived at the bus stop in time to meet the bus. We both started walking back home down the country road whilst wheeling my bike. She was telling me all about her days adventure in Chatswood about the movie she had just been to see. I was listening with great enthusiasm and looking forward to the same opportunity that would come my way one day. About half way home, a car came past us, it then turned around and came back towards us again. Neither of us were really surprised as people were often lost, sometimes they would stop to get directions. As the car passed us the second time, it stopped and a man got out of the car and walked quickly towards us. My sister asked him if he was lost but he ignored her, in a flash he produced a big knife from behind his back and went for my sister's head, I was speechless as he started to cut one of my sister's long plaits off!

The sight of the big knife was more than enough for me... I

dropped my bike and ran down the road as fast as I could. I was at least two hundred yards away before I regained some sense of composure. I turned around and started to run back as fast as I could to where my sister was still standing by my bike which lay in a heap on the road where I'd dropped it. The man had gone and my sister was just standing there crying. She had one plait hanging down her back, the other had been cut off close to her neck.

I was shocked, I had no idea why this had happened. She was shaking and crying. After some time, I picked up my bike and we started to walk again. I suppose the most incredible thing was that Margie had managed to memorise the number plate of the car. All the way home, we both repeated the number over and over again until we finally arrived at the house. My sister told Mum what had happened. Shocked, she rushed into the house to call the police on the phone that had been recently connected. The police arrived several hours later in a police car, but neither were dressed in uniforms just city suits. They stood around asking loads of questions. After their questioning, a newspaper reporter arrived wanting to take photographs and asking loads more questions. He told mum that the paper would run the story in the next edition.

A picture of my sister ended up on the front page, I remember seeing the newspaper article with her photo! On the next page there was a small cartoon of two little pigs with curly tails. The caption read… "We better watch out, I hear someone's going around cutting off pigtails."

The next day the police phoned my father and said Margie must have got the number plate wrong as the one she'd given them belonged to a truck. My father insisted she was correct, about two weeks later they caught the man red-handed with

Margie's plait still stuffed under the front seat! The number plate on the car was correct, it had been stolen from someone's truck. The culprit apparently was employed in a cinema in the Sydney suburb of Collaroy, where three weeks earlier, another little girl had had her hair cut off in the same manner in the cinema where he worked.

This short story just shows how fear can control you. In my case, I had been so scared at the time, I ran away.

"FIGHT OR FLIGHT."

Chapter 8

The Baker

One day, a neighbour came to the farm to use the phone. While turning his vehicle around he accidentally ran over and squashed one of the chicken's water troughs. The water troughs were galvanised and were made up to be semi-automatic — supplying water to the chickens in a little tray at the side. They would last several days before having to be refilled again, the cost was significant. Knowing my father's reputation of being bad-tempered, he slung the squashed water trough into the bush in order not to be found out.

Some days later, my father found the water trough in the bush, squashed and damaged beyond repair, he was very angry. After some thought as to whom it might have been, he assumed that the only person who had come to the farm recently had been the baker.

In those days bread, milk and groceries were all delivered to the house. When the baker came the following week, my father was waiting for him.

I was probably about five at the time, but I can remember the whole scene as though it was yesterday. When the baker pulled up in his little van, I was playing in the dirt nearby. The baker got out and went to the back of his van and opened the two small doors where a large basket of bread was. He was preparing the bread that was in the bread basket for the delivery, my father saw his opportunity, and went for him like a madman yelling and shouting. The baker ran around the van and desperately climbed back into the driver's seat, at the same time trying to lock the doors.

The poor man had no idea what was going on, by that time my father had the baker's crank handle in his hand and was waving it about wildly accusing him of running over the water trough that he'd found squashed in the bush, he continued to shout at him to get out and fight. The poor baker just wanted to get the hell out of there. The baker managed to lock both front doors and was trying to start the van. My father was still trying to rip one of the side doors open. Not having any success, he decided to go to the back doors that were still open. He started to pull out all the baker's bread from the big basket and also grabbed his money bag. He tipped the basket of bread out into the dirt, and then went through the money bag taking out the approximate cost of the water trough. He then slung the bag and the balance of the money back into the back of the van, then he tipped the bread that was still in the basket out onto the dirt and kicked it all around until it was ruined. By that time the baker had got his van going. He was not about to get out of the van and retrieve his basket. The last thing I saw was the baker speeding down the old farm track in his van with both back doors swinging uncontrollably with my father still running behind him! The baker, needless to say, never returned! Later, we found out that the visiting neighbour had run over the water trough not the baker. It just goes to show how anger can get in the way of rational thinking.

"LEFT BRAIN THINKING!"

Chapter 9

Toilet Paper

On the farm, our outside toilet, or outhouse as it was commonly called, was a soil toilet which had to be emptied when full. Ours was quite close to the house, as they usually were. When the time came to empty it, a big hole had to be dug. It was one of the jobs we boys took in turns to do. It had a toilet drum cylinder with a seat, which slid over another drum which had two handles. If it was allowed to get too full, it was very heavy and would slop when carried. A hole would have to be dug for the effluent to be tipped into. When the drum was tipped into the hole, we had to stand back so as not to get splashed. Sometimes an unsuspecting sister got it in the face, it was all good fun and part of farm life.

When I was about eight years old, I was very prone to day dreaming. One day when I was sitting on the throne — as it was called, I got a bit carried away with the amount of toilet paper I was supposed to use. In other words, I just kept pulling the paper off the roll that was nailed to the toilet wall. Why? I don't know, it was just something little boys do. Later when my father went to use the toilet, he saw all the paper crunched up inside. He got very angry and pulled all the paper out of the toilet, not just my paper but every bit of paper he could get his hands on. He draped it all across the low tree branches everywhere, just high enough for me to reach it. There it stayed until it was dried but still filthy. I had to use the second-hand toilet paper every time I went to the outhouse, one square at a time until it was all gone!

People would come to the farm to buy chickens from time to time as we used to sell chickens to the public, several regular customers remarked to Mum, "What is all the filthy toilet paper doing there?" My embarrassed Mum would then have to explain. Our push bikes were our only escape, so taking them away from us was really clipping our wings. For some misdemeanour, I can't even remember what it could possibly have been, my father chained all three bikes to a gum tree. There they stayed for nearly a year rusting away. It's hard to understand why somebody would do such things.

"We all see things through different windows... It's easy to make a misjudgment."

"THE WRONG PUNISHMENT."

Chapter 10

Alopecia

When I was about ten years old, Mum took me to the doctor to see why I had a bald patch on the back of my head that wouldn't go away. At first, they thought it was ringworm, but eventually after many tests, a specialist took a look at it and told her it was Alopecia — a condition caused by extreme stress. He asked my mother if there was any stress at home. She explained the situation with my father and how he mistreated us all and how he was a tyrant and a bully.

"There lies the problem," the specialist said, "It's a nervous condition." My brother also suffered with a nervous sniff until his mid-twenties for the very same reason. We were all so scared of my father because we never knew when he was going to lash out at us. We were taught not to speak until spoken to, and we were never allowed to speak during an adult conversation.

At dinner time around the table there was always a bad feeling, there was no way to relax… If we wanted something, like the butter or the salt and pepper, we always had to ask for anything to be passed to us, even if we could quite easily reach it. We would have to ask, "May I have the salt please," or, "Would you pass me the butter please." If the item on the table was close enough you didn't have to ask.

There was an invisible line that only my father could see, and if one reached across that invisible line without asking, an enormous hand would come crashing down on your face. Worse than that, the invisible line seen only by my father, seemed to change position according to his mood! No one was allowed to leave the table until my father had finished, and even then, we had to ask to be excused no matter what the reason.

He once threw a kerosene tin at my brother when he was six years old because he was not working hard enough; my brother still has the scar on his head.

My sister was dragged around the veranda by her hair and arm, left bruised and bleeding before she went to her first new job, she was just seventeen.

I envied her for at least she could get away some times. I can remember being picked up and thrown into a wood heap trying to out run my father.

He was a maniac, and beatings were a common thing, verbal abuse and ridicule continued all the time. It wasn't only us children, my mum got it as well; she sometimes had black eyes and a bleeding head from his abuse. Mum was our rock and without her I don't know how we would have survived. She stayed with him only for the sake of us children.

One day Mum invited a couple of friends to dinner. Sometime during the dinner, the man made some complimentary remark toward Mum, my father took offence to it and beat him black and blue as well!

"EMOTION CAN EASILY CONTROL US."

Chapter 11

In The Poo

By the 1960's, business was starting to pick up with the introduction of dressed chickens being supplied to restaurants and shops alike. A new processing shed was built with two cool rooms — one of which was in fact a freezer. A new plucking machine was purchased, along with two fibreglass vats which were filled with ice to chill the freshly dressed chickens quickly.

There simply was too much work, so my father decided to hire help, it came in the form of young country boys who came to the farm and lived at the farm. My father supplied bunk accommodation, while poor Mum was given an extra workload of cooking all their meals plus doing their washing! For this service, the boys would pay three pounds a week out of their wages, but it was never enough money for Mum to make ends meet, so she got the bright idea of putting in a cigarette machine, as in those days everybody seemed to smoke.

My father employed about eight or ten farm workers, most were aged eighteen to twenty-two, there was very little to do for recreation for the boys. I was just thirteen, you can just imagine how much I was teased and taunted. It was never possible to get them back for their constant teasing, and by the age of thirteen, I had left school and was working full-time on the farm.

Most of the chickens we had were in cages, so their manure had to be removed constantly. We would scrape and shovel it all into a trailer which was pulled along by a motorised tractor. On the back of the trailer was a small platform where one person could sit, while the trailer was taken to another part of the farm to be offloaded.

One day a farmworker, a nineteen-year-old named Billy Gosling, was working with me. We had just finished loading the trailer full of sloppy manure and were proceeding to the next paddock to offload it. Instead of sitting on the back, he stood on the small platform with hands on his hips, showing off... I was driving the tractor which had a hand clutch, the clutch had two positions, one for going forward, and the other back for parking. I was driving quite slowly when I looked back at him standing there. I thought I'd have some fun with him, as he had been ribbing me for a long time.

The week previously at lunch time he and the other boys had played a dirty trick on me. They had opened my sandwich and placed some dry foul manure in it while I was busy looking at some distraction. I had fallen hook, line and sinker into their joke... I returned to eat my sandwich and took a large bite. The moment I swallowed the first mouthful they all broke out laughing. Suspicious of what happened, I opened the sandwich to find that most of the manure had gone down my neck.

'Today,' I thought to myself, 'was get back time.'

We were driving on a moderate incline when I released the clutch, Billy momentarily leaned forward but regained his balance. I then put the clutch back in, of course the tractor lurched forward again. Billy momentarily went back, but again regained his balance... however at that moment, he still had a certain amount of forward momentum, so I released the clutch once happier to see Billy plungè headfirst with arms spread out straight into the sloppy manure! I quickly put the tractor into gear again and jumped off leaving it driverless and still heading up the paddock! As I sprinted from the scene, I heard shocking expletives coming from Billy — who was by now busy wiping himself off and trying to regain control of the driverless tractor. I knew he would have to do this so for a moment I knew I was safe. It felt good to finally get a bit of my own back, but all too soon I realised that he would beat me up when he saw me next.

"EVERYBODY GETS THEIR OPPORTUNITIES AT SOME STAGE, EVEN IF IT'S A LITTLE SWEET REVENGE."

Chapter 12

Daydream

Depression is not something I'm prone to, in fact I'm a very positive person, but in those days, depression came only too often. I once contemplated shooting myself as I'd had enough of my father constantly ridiculing me and telling me I was a bloody idiot, and many other expletives that shouldn't be printed! He would also beat me around the head and anywhere else he could reach, it was a terrible time for me, shooting myself seemed a logical conclusion.

As kids we were all trained to use a rifle, because there were so many snakes and vermin to be kept under control. This meant I had the rifle and I had the bullets. I was eleven at the time. It's hard to imagine that things were so bad on the farm, but they were. I didn't feel I had anything to live for.

Then one day when I was supposed to be working, as kids do, I went into a bit of a daydream. Standing in the sunshine and feeling very depressed, I had what you might call a vision. I saw myself with a little girl, and I thought this doesn't make any sense, because I was only a young boy myself. But there I was looking down and holding the hand of a little girl. Somehow, I knew that this was very important, and also that it was my future. I suddenly realised there and then, that there was a lot more of life to come for me. It was very strange because I was standing up, I wasn't asleep and yet in my mind's eye, it was as clear as if it was really happening right then. Of course I know now it was a premonition, and one of many more still to come to me.

This particular premonition was sent to me to tell me that I was only thinking about myself, and not considering the future at all… In fact, it saved my life.

I think it's very sad when young people lose their way, and consider or commit suicide. Be patient, you will see that there is much more still to come for you with numerous opportunities.

I hear people often say, "Gee, you're lucky," or, "I never had anything like that happen to me." Well, everybody gets numerous opportunities in their life but most people unfortunately don't notice them, and those that do are often so fearful of stepping out of their box that they won't have a go. Life is only a 'play' after all. When we are born, we step onto the stage, when we die we step off again.

This daydream I had pulled me back from my dark thoughts, and so the rifle and the bullets were put away out of my mind.

"EVERYTHING IS HAPPENING AT THE SAME TIME IN THE ABSOLUTE REALITY… PAST, PRESENT AND FUTURE."

Chapter 13

A Pound Note

When I was about twelve, I was allowed to go to the cinema for the first time on my own. It was a big deal catching the bus on my own and going to Chatswood all by myself. I felt like a young man.

But as little boys do, I decided to hitch-hike home to save my bus fare from the return trip. It was a mistake I came to regret, but it was the only way I could get some pocket money.

It was usually very easy to get a ride in those days, so on this occasion when a car stopped, I just climbed in. I was very interested in cars in those days, and recognised the model and name of this particular vehicle straight away as a Vanguard space master. It was pink and white with a blue stripe down the side. I remember the vehicle like it was yesterday, some things you never forget.

We drove for a while and the man behind the wheel seemed quite talkative and friendly. What is now a built-up suburb was then quite rural and bushy. He said to me, "Do you want to earn a pound, boy?" I had never had a pound note before; that was a lot of money for any twelve-year-old who had been saving and treasuring his sixpences from saved bus fares. I answered innocently, "Yes", thinking he wanted me to help him do something perhaps on his car. He chose a bushy area and turned off up a little track.

I had no idea what was about to happen. He gave me the pound note and then said to me, "Open your fly." I was used to doing what I was told by my father, or I would be in serious trouble, so I did as he asked. He reached over and started to touch me, then when he lowered his head I thought, 'What's he going to do, was he going to kiss me there?'

I had no idea what was going on, I can remember thinking, 'I've got to get out of here,' but I was too scared to move. Being only twelve years old I didn't react like he'd expected, so he gave up after a while. Then he started massaging himself. I had never seen anything like it.

I was very scared and I just wanted to run but was too afraid to move, so I just sat there. Eventually he wiped himself with a hanky when he was finished. He then told me to zip up my fly and asked if I wanted to do this again next week. When I said in a frightened voice, "No," he told me to get out of the car. I watched him drive along the bush track until it met the road, where he drove away never to be seen again. I was left dumbfounded standing on the dirt track in the bush.

After a while I decided to walk the last six miles to the farm. There would be no more hitchhiking for me. It's an experience I've never and will never forget. I think that it probably happens more often than people realise, but most people are too ashamed or too embarrassed to talk about it.

I am seventy-two now and I am just talking about it for the first time. As the years went by, I did still hitchhike from time to time, but I was always very careful what car I got into. It made me very wary.

"EVERY PLAY HAS THE BAD GUY IN IT."

Chapter 14

Runaway

Back on the farm at around the age of thirteen, I was so unhappy and disillusioned that I decided to run away from home. Very little planning went into leaving, I just packed a few things in a suitcase and set off very early one morning.

There was only one road out from the farm and it took me in the wrong direction to where I had intended to go. So I decided to take a bush track as I thought it might trick my father... I knew he could easily catch me if I took the road.

My decision made I decided to cut down through the bush, which was quite a long walk carrying a suitcase. I also had the disadvantage of a river to cross, but I was sure I could do it so off I went.

I left early before anybody was awake. I took a can of sweetened condensed milk, a loaf of bread, some matches, and a ten-shilling note. The bread was okay, but most of it was gone by the time I got to the river... I had also forgotten the can opener, so there would be no condensed milk!

After about three hours of walking, I reached the river. I thought I could wade across as it wasn't too deep, but I was wrong. I had misjudged the fact that this part of the river was still affected by tide, and there were very deep holes. As I waded out, the water soon came up to my neck, and eventually I had to swim with my suitcase in tow. By the time I got to the other side of the river, my suitcase was not floating very well. After clambering out of the water on the other side of the river, I opened the suit case and discovered that it was half full of water and all my worldly belongings were soaked.

Still confident of my escape, I decided to ring all my clothes out and hang them on trees in the sun to dry them. It was lunchtime by the time I was on my way again. I walked on until I found the main road where I started to hitchhike north. God knows what I must've looked like, any wonder it took ages to get a lift. I had no destination in mind — I just wanted to get away.

After two days of sleeping rough I was really hungry. An opportunity arose where I was able to steal a fowl from someone's back yard. Hiding in the bush I waited until it was dark, then I carefully crept to where the fowls were nesting. I quietly picked one up and immediately wrung its neck to silence it! This came easily to me as I had done it many times before on the farm. With dinner in hand, I slipped away from the house and returned to my little hideaway in the bush. I felt like a thief in the night, and even though I was a little apprehensive about my future, I also felt proudly confident. I lit a small fire, and after plucking the foul, I proceeded to try and cook the thing holding it over the fire with green sticks, it turned out to be burned on the outside and raw on the inside. But it was food and that was all that mattered at the time.

With a full tummy, I soon fell asleep only to be woken early with droplets of rain. Some doubt started to creep in at that stage; I was beginning to wonder if I had made the right decision to leave home.

After spending most of the following day standing on the side of the road unable to get a lift, I decided to walk. It was almost dark when I finally found a spot to sleep. It was a grassy spot, near a bridge. I decided that it would do. I settled down with my suitcase beside me on the grass exhausted, I was soon fast asleep.

Some hours later I awoke in pitch darkness to find my suitcase floating in about three inches of water. I quickly realised that the spot I had chosen was tidal and I was very wet. I hadn't noticed it before as I had been so tired.

Almost in tears, I dragged my bag of wet belongings out of the water and up the bank. I had to get moving again even though I was wet, tired, and hungry. I had no choice but to push on — to pour salt on my wounds, it started to rain again!

Eventually I came to a town… I have no idea what it was called, but in the middle of the main street there was a public toilet. I ran to it to get out of the rain. It must have been around one or two o'clock in the morning. I sat down on the cold tiled floor and instantly fell asleep. It seemed no time at all when I opened my eyes to the sound of someone yelling at me. It was a big policeman, he was saying, "Get up! You're coming with me." I was petrified, I didn't know what to do, but all of a sudden, the policeman's car radio sounded. He walked over to the car and spoke into the microphone and then he looked at me and said, "You wait here, I'll be back for you shortly." Lucky for me he got called away to something more important. I saw my chance, as soon as he was gone, I grabbed my bag and ran like crazy down the main street until I was back on the highway. I was suddenly very much awake. The sky seemed to be brightening up, it was almost day break.

Somehow, I managed to make it all the way to Taree. In those days that was two hundred and ten miles from Sydney on a very winding road. It took about a half a day or more to drive from Sydney, but for me, it had taken nearly three days. On arrival in

Taree, I needed to get a job and some money. I didn't want to look like I was just passing through, so I hid my bag behind a service station before setting off to look for a job. I managed to get a lift to an industrial area. I walked around and eventually found a truck loading dock. They were loading bags of potatoes, I managed so I thought, to secure a job to start the following day. All I had to do now was find somewhere to eat and sleep. Unbeknown to me, my accommodation and food had already been arranged, for when I came out of the truck dock, a police car was parked outside.

Two big policemen were standing there — one said to me, "Get in the back," while the other one held the back door of the car open. I was really very afraid — I didn't know what to expect next. I must have appeared feral from their point of view. I had been in the same clothes for three and a half days and sleeping out in the bush I'd not had a proper wash. I can only guess what I looked like. I was so afraid my father would now find out where I was. I fell back into the seat of the car as it took off — strangely enough it was the most comfortable place I had been in since I left home. The policemen began asking me questions like what my name was, where I came from, and what I had been doing. They finally asked me where my things were and I told them I had left my bag behind the service station. They picked my bag up for me and then took me to the police station. I was so frightened as they made me sit for hours while they went on with other things. It seemed to take forever. Looking back at what had happened, I realised that the man at the truck bay had called the police realising that I was an underage runaway.

Today if a thirteen-year-old ran away from home, a social worker would be called in to assist, but in those days, the runaway was considered a naughty little boy who should be returned home immediately to face the consequences from his father. Eventually I was taken into the prison block. The cells were all full so I was left in the hallway in front of the cells — the toilet was at one end. The walls were made of brick and the floor concrete, it was a dismal cold place.

The three full cells had what I considered hardened criminals in them. They all looked at me, eventually one of them asked, "What are you in for?" I answered, "Running away from home," at which they all laughed. One of them then asked, "Got any durries?" A durry was a common country term for a roll your own cigarette in those days. "No," I answered. These men frightened me. I was too scared to make eye contact so I just sat on the concrete floor with my head down between my knees. Sometime later, a policeman came to the door and I was handed a plate of food. I can't remember what it was, but I scoffed it down like some sort of a wild animal.

I was very careful not to get too close to the other cells, the three men in these cells looked really dangerous and bad to me.

Sometime later the door opened again and someone threw a blanket at me. That was it until the next morning. I had to sleep on the cold concrete without even a board of wood to lie on.

During the night it got very cold, and I was awake most of the time curled up with my blanket. In the morning I awoke to the sound of the other prisoners talking. I wondered if it had all just been a bad dream, but it wasn't, as I realised I was sore and aching.

For some reason unknown to me, I was taken outside onto the grass lawn. The sun was shining and I suddenly had a wonderful appreciation for it. I sat in the sun for about half an hour, and then a man came out with breakfast for me. It was one of the nicest meals I've ever had — eggs on toast and a cup of hot tea! Relaxing in the sun with a full tummy, I soon fell asleep.

It was nearly lunchtime when I heard my mother's voice. I thought at the time she was very angry with me, as she was crying, but I realised later she was crying with joy to see me. The police had called my home after extracting the necessary information from me the night before, but they hadn't told me Mum was coming to pick me up. Driving back home in the old Ford Prefect, I asked her what my father had said and what he was going to do to me.

She replied that he had said, "Leave the bastard there."

"DESPERATE PEOPLE TAKE DESPERATE MEASURES."

Chapter 15

Bonnie & Bobby

My sister and I always wanted a horse on the farm, but it had been strictly forbidden. For years we begged and pleaded, but my father would not allow us to have one. Fortunately for me, the farm became busier and busier, and my father had to employ some live-in workers. They were young men who were about eighteen to twenty years old mostly. They were from the country and were used to having horses for their recreation. As there was nothing much to do in the area, my father allowed them to get a horse each. My sister and I continued with our pleading, eventually with Mum's persuasive help, he relented... I was fourteen at the time.

This was one of the best things that ever happened to me while I was living on the farm. I bought my first horse with money I had saved, since I was working full time. She was called Bonnie, she was about thirteen hands high, chestnut in colour with a beautiful long two-toned mane of chestnut and blonde. She had very long eyelashes, surrounding the most beautiful eyes, she also had a wonderful nature. She became my escape... I rode her everywhere bareback as I couldn't afford a saddle, we had lots of good times together. I built her a nice stable out of scrap material from the farm. When I fed her at night, I would brush and talk to her, sharing my sorrows, often in tears. She would rest her head on my shoulder and it would become heavier and heavier as she relaxed. She responded to my sadness by shedding loads of tears herself that would run down the side of her face. She seemed to understand, it was amazing, and so our relationship became very close.

As time passed and I grew, I realised I had become too heavy for her as she was really only a pony. Eventually I was forced to sell her, what a sad day that was, it was like losing a very close friend.

About a year later I found another horse locally. His name was Bobby, everybody advised me not to buy him because they said he had a bad nature and would bite and kick. This was true at the time. Running true to form, only listening to myself, I decided he would be right for me, so I went ahead and bought him. Bobby was a part Arab Galloway, steel grey with dapples. I remember getting him home for the first time and trying to put a saddle on him. He immediately turned around ready to bite me. I told him there and then, "Don't do that!" With ears right back he just looked at me, showing the whites of his eyes. I talked to him kindly and brushed him a lot. Within a couple of weeks, I started to see a big change in his attitude. After a while I could do almost anything with him! There was no kicking, no biting, just good behaviour. He had been previously ill-treated, that was when I realised he had developed his biting and kicking habits. He was very skinny, but he soon started to put on weight — he and I become very close friends.

After a couple of months, local people that knew of his history were very surprised at his transformation. He and I spent every available moment together. We had such a good time together, we were virtually inseparable. I could see the care I was giving him was paying off. He began holding his head up high like he was proud of himself. It was very rewarding for me.

In those days my father had leased part of the farm to a contractor. One day unbeknown to me, Bobby got out of the paddock and went down to the chicken sheds to try some chicken feed! He stuck his nose into one of the chicken troughs and started to chew away. I had been out at the time and when I returned, I was told by the contractor that my horse had been eating chicken feed.

About three days later when I was riding Bobby, he slipped on some wet grass and broke his back leg in a most severe way. My sister rushed in to the house to phone the vet. It was about forty minutes before he finally arrived. Poor Bobby was standing there on three legs shaking with shock and obviously in a lot of pain. I was also in shock as I knew there was no way of saving him. He was going to have to be put down. I was crying and extremely upset, I was sixteen at the time. The vet who was only very young, about twenty-four, with very little experience, gave Bobby a lethal injection. Bobby fell to the ground — but seconds later he struggled to his feet again, I could hardly believe it.

His leg bone had split in the fall, a massive jagged bit of leg bone about a foot long, was sticking straight out through his flesh! It was the most horrible thing I had ever seen. I screamed at the vet, "Quickly give him another shot!" By this time the vet was shaking and fumbling trying to reload another injection. Eventually he managed it and Bobby fell dead on the ground. It was one of the most distressing few minutes I have ever been through in my life.

I discovered much later that the contractor had shot Bobby in the leg three days earlier using a solid bullet, not fine rat shot that should have been used to frighten him away. I went to my father and told him in the hope that he might say and do something to the contractor, but all he said was, "It serves you right, you bloody fool." I seemed to be surrounded by heartless, cruel people. I thought I would never get over Bobby's death, but of course you do... Time heals everything.

At night time on the farm, I was sent out to catch the stray fowls that had escaped during the day. After dark the escapees would huddle together, so all you had to do was just quietly place a specially made round wire trap over the huddle then pick them up. They could then be returned back to their appropriate cages.

One particular night, about three months after Bobby's death, I was out catching the escapee fowls.

It was a moonlit night so much so that the trees were casting a shadow. Something caught my eye and I looked up. What I saw at that moment was quite astounding. Down the hill came Bobby cantering towards me! He looked magnificent and in the best of health holding his head up high and lifting his front legs in a prancing manner. I couldn't believe what I was seeing. I was confused and thought immediately, 'He's not dead after all.' I called out his name as I started to run toward him. He stopped cantering down the hill about fifty metres away from me, as I came closer to him, he turned abruptly, reared a little, and cantered back up the hill where he had come from. There, he somehow, just disappeared, it was like he cantered away into nothingness. I ran up the hill for some distance, but he was nowhere to be seen, I'll never forget that moment.

His appearance was a little bit transparent, I know now he had come back to thank me, and to reassure a very distressed sixteen-year-old boy, that he was okay.

The love felt between two souls doesn't have to be human to human, it can quite easily be human to animal, as we are all part of the ONE.

"A WONDERFUL CARING GESTURE!"

Chapter 16

A Lost Love

When I was twenty-two, I went to Europe for an extended trip. I travelled all over southern Europe for six months ending up in Germany. I had run out of money, all I had left was my airfare back to Australia, which was in the bank back home. It was a situation of flying home, or staying in Europe and using my airfare up, in the hope of getting a job.

I had a VW car which I was sleeping in. I used to drive out to the Frankfurt airport where I would sit watching the planes come and go. I really wanted to work for an airline but I had absolutely no experience and couldn't speak German. I would walk around the airline counters and ask if there were any jobs going, but of course that wasn't the way to do it really, especially in Germany, I only had farm experience anyway.

One day, in desperation, I went to the German employment Centre. It was very difficult as practically nobody could speak English and I couldn't speak German, but I did manage to tell one person that I wanted a job with an airline.

He told me to come back the next day, when I did, he gave me a slip of paper with a phone number on it. I called the number straight away and spoke to the manager of the Air Canada freight department. He spoke English well and told me to come and see him.

I got in my little VW and drove straight out to the airport for the interview. He would not commit himself one way or the other, but I was completely out of money, and didn't want to use my airfare unless I was sure I had a job, so I called him almost every day. I annoyed him so much I think, that he eventually said okay, you can start by sweeping the warehouse every day. It wasn't what I wanted but I didn't give a damn, I was that happy to get a job. I was now able to send for my airfare so that I could get a flat as I had been sleeping in the VW and it was almost winter. I remember during the night at the caravan park where I had been parked, I would have to start the little VW up, about every ten minutes or so, so that I would not freeze to death; it's a wonder I wasn't kicked out of the caravan park.

I ended up working for Air Canada for a little over two years. In that time, I worked my way up from sweeping the warehouse floor to supervisor. It was a great experience, I was able to get discounted fares enabling me to travel to many different countries. I was also able to get my parents incredibly good cheap airfares, but my mother was the only one who took up that opportunity. I got her tickets to numerous countries, and one big ticket in particular went right around the world with TWA.

When I was working for Air Canada, I was working shifts, as a result I often had five or six days off at a time. It was my intention while away from Australia to see as much of the world as I could, so every time I had a break I would endeavour to get away.

On one occasion, I travelled to Amsterdam since it was just a thirty minutes flight from Frankfurt and the flight was almost free. I arrived there and stayed in a male hostel. I awoke the next morning to hear movement in the bunk above me and I'll never forget what came over the side of the bed… I had just opened my eyes and saw two beautiful brown legs appear over the side of the above bed, and don't forget I was only twenty-two at the time. Down jumped the most beautiful girl I had ever seen. I said hello as she went over to her boyfriend, who I later found out was her husband. Her name was Sandra, his was Rick. They had been forced to stay in the male section as they'd arrived late the previous night and the female section had been full.

We became good friends and we decided to hire some mopeds. We had a great time and I will never forget her. Sandra and Rick had just arrived in Amsterdam and were intending to buy a car to travel in. I asked them if they would be traveling through to Germany and invited them to visit me.

I couldn't get her out of my mind. Under different circumstances I would have gone to Mars to be with her. I flew back to Germany with my heart aching knowing I had fallen in love with a married woman. I tried to put her out of my mind, as I would never come between two people that were married.

Some weeks later to my delight, they turned up at my little flat in Frankfurt. I was so excited and so pleased to see them, especially Sandra. They stayed a couple of days and then continued on with their travels. I managed to get their address in Atlanta, Georgia in the USA before they left.

Sandra worked for Eastern Airlines in the USA. This beautiful woman was on my mind constantly, I knew I just had to see her again.

About six months later, I had a couple of weeks off and an opportunity to fly to the U.S. on a discounted fare. I flew to Canada and made my way down to Atlanta without telling them, as I wanted to surprise them. The whole of my trip flying over to the U.S. had been full of apprehension wondering if I was doing the right thing, but it didn't matter, I had to see her again. When I arrived, I found out they were away on vacation — bad timing.

The neighbour told me they were expected back in about a week's time. I was very disappointed, but I just had to wait.

I stayed for a day or two with their kind neighbour, and once Sandra's parents realised I had come all the way from Germany to see them, they came and picked me up and I stayed with them for a few days until Sandra and Rick eventually returned. Her parents were really friendly and took me everywhere.

I only had about four or five days with Sandra and Rick before I had to return to Germany. We went out quite a bit, but mostly we just sat around and talked. On one occasion we went to a country barbecue where most of the people were friends of Ricks.

It was a lovely place with a great big lake and a ski boat. There were about twenty to twenty-five people at the barbecue and there was a great big bowl of dope on the dining room table for everyone to help themselves to. I declined and felt a little out of it because I assumed everybody smoked, but to my surprise Sandra said, "I don't smoke either!" Everyone else got stoned and I finally had a chance to talk to her on her own.

I didn't need to tell her how I felt as I'm sure she had already picked it up. No advances were made by me or her, and I had to leave it at that, but before returning to Germany I asked her if I could have a photograph of them. What I really wanted was a photograph of her, to my surprise she gave me a nice photo of her alone.

I left and went back to Germany knowing there was nothing I could do and unfortunately, I never saw her again. I carried her photo for almost twenty years, but eventually I lost hope and gave up.

Forty-three years later, I awoke one morning from a dream. The dream was so vivid that I was in tears, as she had come to me once more.

I dreamed of her not as I last saw her, but as she must have been now. I instantly recognised her although she was much older. I saw her in some sort of a home with writing above each room such as 'Dining Room' and 'Lounge Room'.

I saw people in white shorts, socks and shirts. Someone asked if I would like to see Sandra, they told me to wait outside and she would come to me which she did. I somehow knew that something was wrong. I told her how much I had loved her and how in my thoughts, she had been with me all those years. I told her how happy I was that she had cared enough to want to see me once more.

I had the strange feeling that she had already passed and so I asked her if she had suffered, to which she replied, "Somewhat." I knew she had come to say goodbye. I realised when I awoke that she had been in a home of some sort, I think she had just passed away.

It took me forty-three years to find out that she really cared for me after all.

"A LOVE SO STRONG SHE CARED SO MUCH."

Chapter 17

A Vision

On another occasion when I had a dream (I must have been about thirty-eight), I was the observer... (I often am in dreams). I remain totally unaffected, I don't get hurt in any way. In this particular dream, I could see an old DC3 plane flying at very low altitude. It was night time, the plane hit the tops of some trees and burst into flames. I was on the plane just before it crashed.

The face of a well-known person/passenger stood out among the other unrecognisable faces on the plane. He was standing up, and somehow I knew there were drugs involved. In 2014, for the first time, I did some research on the singer's death. It seems this famous singer and others took a flight on a DC3 after doing a show. It crashed shortly after take-off and all were killed. The crash had occurred many years earlier, so in a sense it was a vision.

As I said earlier in this book, past present and future, are all happening at the same time in a sense, it has already been written, it's just a matter of which road we take that determines our set of experiences.

All events have indeed happened in a way, this is why some people are able to receive visions. It can be past, present, or future — it makes no difference. In the spirit world the real world, there is no time. If there is no time, there is no future or past, hence everything is happening NOW.

"SO FOR WHATEVER REASON, I WAS SHOWN."

Chapter 18

A Premonition

A close friend of mine was staying at my home in Melbourne, I was about forty at the time. One morning over breakfast, I was telling her about a strange dream I had the previous night. I told her that I dreamed about another plane crash, since I've had so many premonitions before, she was not surprised.

She asked me about it, so I told her I'd seen the people on the plane but the plane didn't seem to have wings. It had crashed over what appeared to be the side of a road in a culvert. In the dream I was hovering above looking down at the people, the words kept coming into my head over and over again, "I am so sorry." It felt as though I was responsible for their deaths. It was very clear I was the observer and yet somehow, I was involved but not hurt.

Three days later my friend rushed in with the newspaper and showed me a picture on the front page, it was exactly as I'd described it to her three days earlier in my dream. Instead of a plane, there was a coach on its side in the culvert and nearby was a semi-trailer all smashed up! Reading the article, I noted there had been many people killed on the bus and also the driver of the semi-trailer. It turned out the driver of the semi-trailer had gone to sleep at the wheel, causing all of the deaths of those people on the bus.

I knew immediately that I'd been the driver of the semi-trailer, for a moment in the dream looking down at the coach, I or he, was saying, "I'm so sorry." Those words stuck strongly in my mind... I was there and had been the truck driver; it was very sad.

When I have these dreams, I'm usually the observer and never physically hurt. I seem to be emotionally unaffected.

"I WAS THERE."

Chapter 19

The Windscreen

Years ago on the farm, one of my father's contractors was in the habit of taking his wife each evening to the local shop just up the road, as she didn't drive. This particular night she decided not to go, which was very unusual. It was dark, he was driving back from the shop when a startled horse ran out from behind a bush. It stopped right in front of his oncoming car, reared up and both its front legs went through the windscreen, punching two big holes in the seat where the contractor's wife always sat.

This is more proof that we are being looked after by our spirits or souls. They can see things our physical bodies can't.

"LISTEN TO YOUR MESSAGES!"

Chapter 20

Smiley

Smiley was a runaway Alsatian I found. He had a muzzle on and was hanging around a service station where I usually got my fuel. I asked the station owner who owned the dog, but he said he didn't know and I shouldn't go near him as he had a muzzle on.

Feeling sorry for the dog, I decided to take him home. We advertised for a long time, but no one came to claim him. He became our very good friend and lived with us for the next nine years or so.

In that period, I was always working very hard, I was constantly busy without any time for anything. Sometimes he would just look at me — I couldn't tell what he was thinking of course.

Whenever we had been away for a while, he would greet us on our return with a great big smile showing some teeth! The first time he did it, I thought he was going to bite me as it looked that way.

To cut a long story short, he eventually passed away, I was so taken with him that I made a headstone for his grave and composed a nice poem about him… It went like this:

SMILEY…1989 to 1998
    HE CAME AS A STRAY AND WANTED TO STAY.
    AFTER A WHILE HE DEVELOPED A SMILE WHEN

EVER WE HAD BEEN GONE A WHILE.
THIS BEAUTIFUL BOY WE LOVED HIM SO,
IT WAS SUCH A SHAME WHEN HE HAD TO GO.

My wife's sister who was visiting from the UK at the time, gave me an Azalea as a gift, I asked her if it would be ok to plant it at the end of his grave, she said yes. Many months later I was gardening and noticed that the tie holding the tag was becoming tight as the plant had grown, it had to be removed. Still attached to the plant was a tag which read the Latin name of the shrub, below was the English interpretation.

It was clear to me it was a message from Smiley, trying to tell me to slow down and be more relaxed as he always was.

The translation into English is…

"THE TEACHER!"

Chapter 21

The Tram

When I was about twenty-four, I had a dream about traveling on a tram. In my dream somebody threw half a brick at the tram and it smashed the window where I was sitting. The tram stopped and the driver came back to ask if I was okay. The tram driver chased the culprit, but he ran away and escaped over a picket fence.

The dream was very detailed, I don't remember if I was hurt. As I always I seem to be the observer in these types of dreams.

Thinking about the dream later, I thought it had no particular significance as I didn't know of any place that still had trams operating, other than Melbourne, and I had no intention of going there.

About six months later, my girlfriend and I were traveling through Adelaide where I discovered they had a tram that ran out to the beaches. We decided to go for a ride on it and climbed aboard and sat down.

I had completely forgotten about the dream, but for some reason I said to her, "Let's not sit here, let's sit in the next seat back." We were relaxed and enjoying the trip as the old tram made its way slowly up a slight hill. Then right in front of us the window smashed in as a half brick flew through and landed on the seat right where we were going to sit.

The tram halted and the driver ran back to see what had happened. When I told him, he jumped off the tram and ran after the culprit who subsequently climbed a picket fence and got away!

This is exactly what had happened in my dream. Again, more proof that everything in a sense has already happened, I was being warned, or helped if you like, by my soul/spirit who sees all.

"LISTEN AND ACT."

Chapter 22

Custody

When I was about twenty-five a woman came into my life, she became pregnant with my precious little daughter. About two years after my daughter was born, our rocky relationship ended.

We were living in Cairns at the time, and I was operating a camping safari business taking tourists to Cape York. The idea of starting a safari business had been on my mind for a long time as I love camping and exploring. Although I had the idea at the time I didn't have enough money to start the business on my own, I was forced to make a partnership with another man — a big learning curve!

He and I got along okay at first, but the dirty work was somehow always left to me. It seemed I was always the one underneath the vehicles doing the maintenance and repairs, even after long trips when I was quite exhausted.

The trips varied between five and fourteen days. The business was growing very fast, so after about three years of operating my greedy partner saw dollar signs for himself.

The vehicles had to be prepared and stocked with food water and spare parts. The trips left Cairns and went to Cape York the most northerly tip of Australia, and then returned using a different track. Practically all the tour was over rough tracks with the occasional rough road. Breakdowns were a regular part of the trip, and as a tour operator I was working eighteen or more hours a day, trying to keep a smile on my face, while being pleasant to the customers at all times. It was hard going but rewarding and I enjoyed it very much.

After four years of building the business up from just an idea in my head, the partnership dissolved, and I was taken down financially by my greedy partner. I lost everything due to his clever solicitor and some devious wording in our partnership contract.

After numerous disputes and problems with my ex, including her decision to take our daughter away altogether, I decided against all odds to try for sole custody.

It was 1978 and as a child needs at least one responsible parent I decided to have a go.

In those days trying to find a solicitor to represent my case was near impossible. I went to practically every solicitor in town, I eventually found one who was prepared to take on my case. All the other solicitors said, "Forget it, you haven't got a chance." I asked the new solicitor what he thought my chances were and he told me he'd won custody of his two children, which was good enough for me. I knew it would be very difficult because in those days it was extremely rare for a single father to be awarded custody.

At that stage my daughter was living with me anyhow, all I wanted to do was keep her in a stable situation. My ex, who was only living two blocks away, had only seen her daughter six times in six months, and was always it seems too busy going out and having a good time.

I gave the solicitor the go-ahead, he told me she would be served shortly, I was disturbed about all this but I had no choice. When my ex was served with papers for the court case, she became very angry.

One day she pulled up in her car and tried to take our daughter forcibly from my car. I saw red and prevented her from dragging our little girl, who was screaming and crying by this time — out of the car. She left the scene, later that day she sent her black belt karate boyfriend around! I think she expected him to beat me up and so did I.

I wasn't a physical fighter and wasn't sure how to handle the confrontation, but I stood my ground. Realising that he was a qualified karate expert and his hands were his weapons, the thought that came to my mind was to verbally threaten him instead. Somehow, I conjured up great composure and said to him, "If you lay a finger on me, I will have you in court so quickly you won't have time to scratch yourself." To my amazement he backed off and went away. I look back at that knowing and trusting everything would be okay, and it was.

The court case for the custody was on a Friday and I assumed it would be finalised that day, but it was held over until the following Monday.

Monday was the beginning of a five-day tour, I could see it was going to clash with the court case… I didn't know which way to turn, yet I seemed to be getting help from the most unexpected places. A friend of mine who was a policeman had a day off that coming Monday, I asked him if he could drive our small four-by-four bus up to Cooktown. He told me he could do that, but as he was working shift that evening, he would have to be back in Cairns for work. With the help of a travel agent friend, I obtained an air ticket from Cairns to Cooktown for me, and from Cooktown to Cairns for my policeman friend who had to return for work.

The flight from Cairns left at two p.m., that all sounded like it would work so I told my solicitor about my arrangements, he said, "Don't worry it will be finished by lunch time, we'll have a decision by then." When lunchtime came on the Monday, the court was adjourned again. I was getting very anxious because I had to catch the two o'clock flight out, otherwise a bus load of tourists would be stranded in Cooktown without a tour leader, what a predicament I was in.

So far, the case had dragged on for two days causing me great stress, especially during the hearing when I'd been accused of fabricating the facts. Lunch time came when I said to my solicitor, "I have to go, I can't leave twelve people stranded like this." He said he'd represent me and let me know the outcome.

I caught the plane to Cooktown. On arrival, my friend was parked at the terminal with the bus load of tourists. He got out of the bus, we shook hands, I thanked him.

As he boarded the aircraft, he turned and gave me a wave. I proceeded to the bus and climbed aboard.

"Good afternoon, everybody, my name is Geoff, I will be your tour guide for the next five days." The words came out with confidence as though there was nothing wrong, but inside I was numb with anxiety.

The poor passengers didn't have a clue and probably wondered why we were changing drivers at the airport. I commenced the tour showing people around, taking them to the sites as I had done many times before. I don't know how I managed to concentrate on giving a tour when all I could really think about was the custody case.

Eventually we arrived back in town, I headed straight for the post office where I knew there was a public phone. I said to the passengers, "I have to make an important phone call, I'll be back in a minute or two."

When I climbed aboard the bus again, I was crying with tears of joy! Well, if I hadn't had their attention before, I certainly had it now! I just sat there in the driver's seat and didn't move. My head was spinning and tears of joy were running down my face. I had to say something to them, some sort of an explanation was needed. I turned around and faced them, I told them I had just been through a court case for custody of my precious daughter and just received the news I'd won!

Most of the people on-board were in their fifties to sixties while I was only thirty. I apologised and said to them, "Okay, let's continue with our tour," but one of the women piped up quickly saying, "Oh no you won't, we're going to the pub to celebrate!" Everyone agreed.

I was shocked but I had no say in the matter. Anyhow it turned out a great idea and I certainly needed a drink to calm myself down.

The next five days seemed to go very slowly, but everybody was so friendly, the women took over the cooking which I always did, and treated me like I was their son. It ended up being one of my best trips. Here I was, celebrating the most important event of my life with total strangers. Amazing, isn't it?

If you trust in your personal message and know you are doing what you consider is the best thing, then there should be no doubt and therefore no need to worry. Apprehension creates doubt, and doubt creates worry. As we all know, most of the things we worry about, never happen anyhow.

Looking back now I realise my beautiful little girl was the one I'd seen in my daydream so many years before. Just a bit more proof that everything is happening now, and that it is all written

"TRUST YOUR PERSONAL MESSAGE."

Chapter 23

The Bank Manager

Just before my custody case, I was trying to buy my first house. I had been living in a converted bus which I had fitted out myself. It was very nice and had every convenience, but I felt that it was time to have something more permanent for my daughter.

I had been trying to sell the bus for several months with no success. I needed to sell it to raise some money to help with the deposit for the house I was preparing to buy.

One day I was approached by a man who owned a very nice caravan, he wanted to do a swap to avoid any more payments on his caravan. In other words, if I was to take the caravan over, I would also have to pay the money owing on it to the finance company. I carefully weighed up the pros and cons, although I was getting into debt, I was securing a better more modern vehicle, so we decided to do the swap.

Getting back to buying the house, I went to the bank to see if I could raise a loan, I explained to the bank manager that I had just started a new business, and that any money I earned was being poured back into it — in other words, I had no cash! But I explained I had a fairly nice caravan which had enough equity in it to cover a small loan for the deposit for the house.

It was a big ask, here I was trying to buy a house without any money!

He looked at me and said, "What exactly is it you want?" I

explained I would like to borrow three thousand dollars to cover the deposit for a house, and that I'd pay it back once the caravan was sold. He asked how I intended to make the payments, and I replied it was not my intention to make payments but to pay back the loan immediately the caravan was sold. He said, "This sort of arrangement is not possible," and politely showed me the door. I left the bank feeling very unhappy about the whole thing.

Sitting in my car thinking about it, I thought to myself, 'I'm not taking this... I have to have this loan, I have to buy the house.' I jumped back out of my car and sprinted up the bank stairs again back to the bank manager's office.

His secretary said in a loud voice, "You can't go in there, you don't have an appointment." I retorted, "Don't worry, I won't keep him a minute." As I proceeded into his office, he just sat there looking at me and asked, "What do you want this time?" I replied, "I have to have the loan, I need three thousand dollars to buy this house."

Apparently, he had thought it was pretty brave or bold of me, because he said, "All right, I will give you the loan, but I expect it to be repaid within the first three months."

You can't imagine how excited I was to be able to buy my first home! I rushed downstairs and drove back home to set the wheels in motion for selling the caravan. Over the next few weeks, I purchased the house with the deposit I had just borrowed.

My first house payment was due at the end of the month, my caravan payment was also due and first loan payment for the three thousand dollars was due!

After weeks of trying to sell the caravan on consignment, I was desperate, I had to sell it now. Frustrated and starting panic, I brought the van back to the house in desperation. Everything was coming all at once, I knew if I didn't sell the caravan straight away, I would be in serious trouble.

Listening to my right brain with no logic, I decided to call up some caravan park owners I knew, to see if they might be interested in a caravan to use as an on-site unit, maybe I could get some rent for it I thought.

It was just an idea, but the very first person I called said, "Yes, I'm looking for one right now." Within the hour he was at the house looking at the caravan, he liked it and he pulled out a cheque book straightaway. I was able to get the cheque cashed and make all three payments just a few days before they fell due!

"NEVER TAKE NO FOR AN ANSWER, IF YOU REALLY WANT SOMETHING, GO GET IT."

Chapter 24

Pioneer

After the breakup of our safari business, I worked casually driving a concrete truck for Ready Mix Concrete Company. I was about thirty-three at the time. I knew that there was good money to be made as an owner driver, but the concrete companies were not putting any trucks on at that time.

Cairns was still in its infancy as far as building was concerned; in fact, the first high rise building was yet to be built. One day I received a phone call from the manager of Ready Mix, who I had been working for casually, he told me that there was a new company coming to town. He didn't want to mention any names, as that would have been a conflict of interest, but he told me they may need some owner drivers. This was the opportunity I had been waiting for, it didn't take me long to find out which company it was. I flew to Sydney, went straight to their head office and asked to see the manager. I told him I'd heard they were starting a new concrete plant in Cairns, and they were looking for owner drivers. I also told him I had a truck ready to start. Actually, it was only a guess, I only assumed that they were the new company going to Cairns, and I hadn't even bought a truck at that stage!

However, the ploy worked and the manager asked me, "What type of truck is it?" I knew they mostly used Internationals so I told him it was an International. He then said, "There are two other trucks starting at the new plant, you will be the third one."

It all happened so fast my head was in a spin, he called one of the secretaries over and said, "Get this man a contract." Within twenty minutes I was signing it. He also asked, "When can you be in Cairns?" I answered, "Whenever you're ready." He replied, "Okay, your truck has to be painted in our company colours first." He gave me some company Decals for the doors, and told me to be in Brisbane in four weeks' time to pick up the new agitator from Rheem, (an agitator is the mixer that goes on the back of concrete trucks). I left their office in a panic to say the least.

After losing my four-wheel drive camping business to my greedy partner, I suddenly found I had another good opportunity, I now had to try and find a second-hand truck of the same make and model that I had told the manager at the concrete company.

As I said, if you're on the right track, things fall right into place. Three days later after nosing around at different concrete plants, I found someone who had just bought a new truck and had his old International ready to sell. He had been about to trade it in on the new one, but he said to me, "You can have it if you give me the same amount of money that I can get on the trade-in." I was able to match the price, I had the truck now it was off to the paint shop! A week later I was ready to leave for Brisbane to pick up the agitator.

I worked very hard with the truck, often pouring concrete slabs at four in the morning as it was too hot to pour concrete in the sun in Cairns. That meant twelve-to-thirteen-hour days... it became a regular thing as we had to stay at the plant until four thirty in the afternoon.

During that period, I managed to save enough money to place a deposit on a second house. The two houses were side-by-side, I knew that the zoning was for multi units as it was just two streets back from the beach. I thought to myself with my logical brain, 'I'll be right now, this will set me up.' However, I didn't realise there were other plans for me already a foot.

My daughter was becoming increasingly upset. She was living with me full-time, but her mother was now starting to make a comeback, she was visiting more frequently and taking her a couple of times a week. God knows what she was saying to her, but it was not acceptable to have a child stressed and confused like that... I could see the confusion and stress building up. After the visits she would often come home crying and it would take two or three days for her to settle down again, by which time her mother was back to take her for another day visit. I could see this was not working out so for my daughter's sake I decided something had to be done as I couldn't bear to see her upset all the time.

I decided the only way to fix the problem was to move away. I thought about it long and hard as I knew her mother would not be happy.

In the meantime, one of the drivers at the concrete plant had put his truck up for sale, due to the building trade going a bit quiet. A number of people had looked at his truck and one man in particular intended to buy it for his son, but hesitated on the purchase for some reason, in the mean time someone else bought the truck ahead of him.

Some two weeks later all the drivers were at the concrete plant when the man who had been interested in buying the truck for his son showed up again.

Terry who had just sold his truck, said to me, "Here comes that guy again with his son to buy my truck, but he's too late — serves him right," he said as he walked out to tell him.

As he got up from his chair I said in a half-hearted manner,

"Tell him he can buy mine if he likes." About five minutes later, the man came up to me and said, "I hear your truck is for sale?" Well, I hadn't exactly anticipated that but I replied without really thinking, "Yes, it is." A week later I was unemployed but with a healthy bank balance. I thought it would be a good idea to get things going right away, so a few weeks later, we were off to the UK where we stayed for just under two years. On arrival in the UK, I bought a camper van, we spent the next six months touring right across Europe visiting many countries, it was wonderful. My daughter saw snow for the first time in Italy and loved it. After the tour was over, I returned to London to sell the camper van and get a job.

Back in Australia I had always been self-employed, and so the only other experience I'd ever had working for someone else, was when I worked for Air Canada in Germany about ten years earlier.

I'd heard the courier company DHL sometimes hired people, so I looked up their head office and went to see the manager. He was an American, and I turned up at his office without an appointment with my five-year old daughter in tow (I was 33 then)! It was certainly a very strange way of going for an interview, but that's how I was. I was never daunted by anything, being conventional is not my style. We got along quite well, he made a phone call and told me to go to the airport warehouse and see the supervisor there. I arrived at the warehouse where I met the supervisor, actually there were two of them. They both asked me many questions, and when they found out that I had worked for an airline and was quite knowledgeable with airfreight, I knew I had a good chance.

During the interview, I discovered one of the supervisors was from Australia, he had actually gone to the same school as me!

We hit it off and I was hired.

My beautiful daughter went to school in London where she picked up quite an accent. To this day I don't think she realises how fortunate she has been.

"WHEN YOU'RE ON THE RIGHT TRACK... THE JIGSAW PUZZLE FITS VERY WELL."

Chapter 25

Married Life

In 1982 we returned to Melbourne Australia to live, I started buying and selling secondhand cars, eventually I moved on to secondhand clothes which didn't do very well at all. One day at the markets I produced a piano chair, it sold very quickly and I soon realised that there was a market for small pieces of old furniture. I knew nothing about antiques, in fact I made some monumental screw ups while learning the trade, but it didn't take me long as I was very keen and interested. Before long I had three stalls at Camberwell Sunday markets, another stall at Victoria antique markets, and in yet another stall at Chapel Street Bazaar. Before long I opened my first shop, it was in Hawthorn and had accommodation above which really suited me. I was able to enrol my daughter at the local school which was only walking distance from the shop. We lived above the shop for just under four years; it was a wonderful time for us both. We then moved to the Dandenongs, where we bought a lovely historical house, I restored it over the next twenty years or so — the work never seemed to end!

At the age of forty-two I got married. My daughter and I had always had a very close relationship. As I had brought her up myself, I always thought having a mother figure around would be beneficial for her. I had no idea what was to come.

My daughter had lots of friends and they often stayed over,

she was very happy. When my new wife came along, I decided we would buy a yacht and rent out the house then sail away into the sunset. Ha! Ha! It all sounded great, but I never really considered how my daughter would be affected, or how she may, or may not get along with my new wife and vice versa, I just assumed all would be well.

I thought it would be quite okay to finish her schooling by correspondence lessons. We had talked about who was going to teach her, but I also hadn't really thought it right through. The clashes between the two girls went on and on, and I found myself in an impossible position trying to please both of them.

What a mess I had got myself into and I had taken two innocent people with me... In those first two years of our marriage, there was loads of conflict on the boat.

My next bright move was to suggest that my daughter finish her schooling at a boarding school, even though it went totally against my real wishes, I pushed on with the idea in order to try and save my marriage. It was a mistake which I regretted.

After six months of boarding school, my daughter became even more unhappy. I decided that she should do her last year of school whilst we all lived on the boat in a marina, which meant not moving. I thought that would help matters a bit, but it was still tough for everybody. I just wanted to please them both but the harder I tried the worse it seemed to get.

My daughter eventually finished her year twelve at Bowen high school, some months later we sailed down the Queensland coast to Bundaberg. The sailing was rough and there were numerous breakdowns. The whole thing was a nightmare for all of us. Trying to get some stability back into our lives, I decided we would all stay in Bundaberg for a while.

We looked around carefully at property prices and

subsequently found a house that was in a good position but needed restoration. The only way we could buy the house was to mortgage our home back in Melbourne. I approached a solicitor in Melbourne to raise some private money to buy the investment property in Bundaberg. I realised I was sticking my neck out again, but I felt very confident. I also knew if things went the way I expected we would all come out of this situation better than the one we were currently in, and also better financially. Considering the whole situation, it felt right. The loan went through and we were able to buy the investment property.

The house was an old Queenslander, which meant it was up on stilts and high enough to walk around underneath. It was made of weather board and had four bedrooms, a kitchen without cupboards, a living room and a bathroom. The front veranda had been enclosed with wrought iron, making it look like some sort of prison, but I could see the potential to restore it to its once former glory, so we started on its renovation. This was more my style, I was very comfortable with the whole situation.

In the meantime, my daughter got herself a casual job. Every night we all rode push bikes back to the boat where it was anchored in the Burnett River. It was a very hot and humid summer and nerves were easily frayed in the confines of a small boat. Eventually, enough work had been done on the house to make it liveable.

My daughter was now able to take a room in the house which helped her considerably as she soon found a boyfriend. Things were looking up for all three of us. We had a tight schedule to repay all the money that we had borrowed to avoid the high interest rates, so work went on relentlessly.

During the restoration my wife was called away to the UK unexpectedly for about a month, so rather than biking back and forth to the boat every day, I decided to stay in the house and sleep on the floor as there was no bedroom furniture. While doing the house up I discovered my neighbour, although now quite old and a bit of a drunk, had been a carpenter. He was very helpful with building the front butterfly stairway for the new veranda. We got along quite well, although he was often so inebriated, he was unable to give the best advice.

One morning I was talking to him on the lower level of the house. I told him that I'd had a very scary dream the previous night in which I had seen two legs dangling down over me. Just before waking up I'd been thrashing around waving my hands in a frantic effort to get away from the dangling legs! I told him how much it had unnerved me, then to my surprise he asked in a very nervous voice, "Which room did you sleep in?" I pointed to the room and saw the horrified look on his face. "What's wrong?" I asked, to which he replied with a bit of a stammer... "That's where the guy hung himself!"

"What are you talking about?" I asked. At that stage I'd no idea there had been a hanging in the house. He continued, "Quick come with me and I'll show you the two rope marks." The rope marks over the bearer of the house where the man had hung himself, were directly underneath the room I'd slept the previous night. Now I understood the whole dream, what I had seen was his two dangling legs swinging and twitching. Just goes to show how something bad like that happening leaves a residue somehow.

We got the house finished in record time in just over four months. We had sanded and painted the complete outside of the house, restored the old veranda back to its former glory. We also built a butterfly staircase that were quite fashionable at the turn of the twentieth century. I constructed a nice little picket fence to finish it off, and we brought in some established palms and made a lovely garden. On the inside, we fixed several broken windows, re-fitted the bathroom, polished all the timber floors, painted it throughout and fitted a new kitchen. The place looked fantastic and was a total transformation from what it had been. People used to walk by in the afternoon and just stand and stare at what we had accomplished in such a short time.

"THERE ARE OPPORTUNITIES FOR EVERYONE."

Chapter 26

The Pedophile

We decided as the house had four bedrooms, to lease out each room to itinerant workers. That way we could maximise the rental return so we could meet our repayments. In the meantime, my wife and I had to go to Melbourne to sort out some issues at home.

We had let one of the rooms to a local man who ran a lawn mowing business, he seemed quite reasonable, and when we told him that we were heading south he asked if he could be a caretaker of sorts. It seemed a good idea at the time as he seemed quite reliable, he was to collect the rent and keep an eye on everybody. He was very keen to live at the house which was situated directly across the road from the high school. Every afternoon at about three-fifteen p.m. he would sit on the veranda with a cup of tea and wave and smile at the schoolgirls as they walked by, he seemed to know quite a few of them. I didn't think that much of it as he had a lady friend who often came to visit and she had three daughters.

Occasionally a young girl from the high school would come to visit him. I asked him one day who she was, he said she was his previous girlfriend's daughter, and that he was like a stepfather to her. They would go straight to his room for a while, sometimes I would see him give her pocket money and cigarettes.

One day, two plain clothed police men came to the door, they asked who I was and who the tenants were that lived there. When I told them about the caretaker, they asked if he had any visitors from time to time. I told them about the young girl and they told me to be very careful, then they went without any explanation.

The visit from the police made me very suspicious. I had a feeling that my 'caretaker' had not been working for a long time and perhaps he'd been in jail. It was just a feeling, but I decided to do some investigating, we went to the library and searched through old newspapers to see if anything fitted him.

I discovered that a little over eight years earlier a man from Bundaberg had been sent to jail on pedophilia charges. I wondered if it could have been him. I came up with a theory that he probably was the same person as the pedophile in the newspapers. I told his girlfriend of my suspicions because she had three daughters, the oldest was about twelve. I had to handle the situation very carefully in case I was wrong, but in any case, she simply didn't believe me… in fact she was very defensive of him.

Putting my suspicions aside, we eventually started our long drive to Melbourne. We had an old Land Rover at the time and were towing an even older caravan.

We had just crossed the border from New South Wales to Victoria when the phone rang; it was my old neighbour, the carpenter. He was in quite a flap, he told me that I should come back immediately as the caretaker had been taken away! I couldn't get much more out of him — he was upset or half-drunk — I wasn't sure which, maybe both I thought. We unloaded the caravan into a storage yard, deciding this would be better rather than tow it all the way back to Bundaberg, then we headed back as fast as we could.

When we arrived three days later, my neighbour explained

how the police had come around and chased my caretaker through our house. He had jumped the fence into my neighbour's garden, run up the stairs to the first level and down the hallway with one of the policeman in hot pursuit, then he charged down the back stairs only to be confronted by the other policeman who tackled him to the ground. There was a lot of screaming and yelling before he was handcuffed and taken away in the police car!

My wife and I went to the local police station to see the caretaker to try and work out what had happened. There he was like a caged animal, I asked him what was going on. All he said was that it was some sort of big mix-up. However, it turned out he was the pedophile I had read about in the old newspaper, he had served a prison term of about eight years. The little girl over whom the new charges had been made was the same victim as before, so he was put away once more for another eight to ten years.

After that episode we decided to put the house on the market to see if we could sell it. We managed to sell it quite quickly with a reasonable profit of twenty-two thousand dollars after taking out all of our restoration costs.

"THE CRIMINAL IN THE PLAY!"

Chapter 27

The Yacht

We spent the next year or so sailing the Whitsunday's — a group of beautiful islands off the Queensland coast. It sounds idyllic, but to tell you the truth it was an endless flow of breakdowns. Often, we would barely make it into port, and on arrival I would spend the duration of our stay in the engine room!

I was very stubborn at that time, and couldn't see the brick wall in front of me! We just kept spending all our money trying to fix up this old boat so she would be ready for our dream trip to sail around the world!

We spent every dollar we had on the boat and eventually we had her ready, or so we thought. She looked fantastic with a new cabin, new paint, a good set of sails and a brand-new diesel motor.

My daughter was staying with her mother for a time in Cairns, so it now seemed possible for my wife and I to start our long-planned voyage around the world.

An incredible amount of preparation had taken place from sourcing all the charts for the trip, calculating all the food supplies and purchasing an extra freezer; plus, new batteries for the boat — everything had to be shipshape so to speak. A new GPS was also purchased… The radar had been serviced — sails put in order with new halyards. A host of spares was also considered like tools bits and pieces that we may or may not need, it took years to get it already.

There were four of us on board, my wife and I plus two crew members. Our first stop after clearing Cairns' customs was the Archipelago Louisiade, not far from the Solomon Islands.

The weather forecast was good for the twelve-day crossing from Cairns to The Archipelago Louisiade's. First, we had to negotiate the passage through the Great Barrier Reef before entering the Coral Sea. I had only coastal experience and had never gone as far as the reef let alone navigated through a passage with coral reefs either side and crashing waves that could be seen from the deck.

It was a bright sunny morning when we cleared customs, it took a day to get to the beginning of the passage through the reef, we had left early that morning so it would still be daylight while navigating the passage. That worked out okay and the passage turned out to be not as daunting as I thought, although I could see waves crashing on the reef either side of us! I was thankful at least that we had planned to navigate the passage during the day, couldn't imagine what it would have been like at night. We headed out through the channel to the open sea. The first ten days, although there was quite a large swell, were fairly uneventful. The sailing was fairly good and the wind was consistent as there was no land around to influence it. We were about two days from making landfall — we had been sailing all the way and hadn't used the engine at all. When I decided to run the engine, at first the engine started beautifully, but then after running for only a few minutes it would stop. I tried many times to keep the motor running but it continually stopped after one or two minutes. I eventually traced the problem to the fuel pump, it had a damaged seal which I was unable to repair. A brand new twenty-thousand-dollar motor, hmmm! Not good.

Our plan was to make landfall at a lagoon, these lagoons in this area were naturally totally sealed in, but during the Second World War different navies in particular the US, blasted entrances in the lagoons so they could take their ships in and anchor in totally smooth conditions, almost like a big Marina. This particular lagoon was one that had been altered, it was well known by yachties and was the usual place to make first landfall or a first stop if you like.

I knew that the lagoon where we were to make landfall was extremely remote, we would be lucky to even find a native. I also knew that it was very tricky to enter a reefed lagoon without an engine, and even more difficult to get out! So after much contemplation, I decided to turn the yacht around and head back to Australia. It was a big decision as we had been planning this trip for many years. Here we were on our first leg and had run into a serious problem, we were all very disappointed.

Turning the boat around meant another twelve days at sea without any proper sleep or even rest. The two young crew did not want to return to Australia, they lost interest totally. They were both inexperienced and turned out to be very lazy and unreliable. This meant my wife and I were on duty practically all the time running on adrenaline. Luckily for us the weather stayed fine, but a big swell was still running.

On about the seventeenth day, one of the crew members that was steering yelled out, "Skipper — we've got no steering!" I was trying to get some much-needed sleep at the time. At that stage it was the last thing I wanted to hear. I ran to the cockpit and took the helm — the wheel was spinning freely with absolutely no control over the rudder. Fortunately for us part of the preparation happened to be the purchase of an emergency tiller. I immediately went to the locker where the emergency tiller arm was kept. Under the aft bed which was the master cabin there was a square block attached to the rudder, in an emergency the aft bed would be pulled to pieces and a large handle placed on the square block that controlled the rudder. When fitted the tiller could be steered or turned from the cockpit thus giving us steering again. We removed the panel under the aft bed and tried to fit the arm directly onto the rudder shaft, but after having it especially made in Cairns, it didn't fit at all! My emotions were a mixture of disappointment and anger, as I had told both crew members on numerous occasions… "Don't swing the wheel from lock to lock," which he had been doing. I said, try and anticipate the boat's heading and steer with small increments of the wheel. The severe swinging of the wheel from side to side had broken a small part in the helm which was not fixable. He was young and headstrong and thought he knew everything! The little voice in my head had told me so many times before we set out not to do the trip, but I hadn't taken any notice.

    Here we were, four to five days from making landfall back in Australia without a motor, and now without steering! We still had to negotiate and navigate the passage through the Great Barrier Reef. It was now looking like we wouldn't even be able to find the passage let alone navigate through it. As well as all this the currents were now pulling us towards the reef at about four knots, it seemed it was just a matter of time before we would hit the reef and break up.

    I called Marine Rescue in Australia on the HF radio to tell them our situation. I would like to say that the Australian Government was helpful, but that wasn't the case at all, we pretty much had to fend for ourselves.

    After many hours on the radio, I received a call from a longline fisherman who'd been listening to our conversations. He told me he would come and tow us back to Cairns, the cost would be twenty thousand dollars. In those days that was a lot of money, and we simply didn't have it. Even in desperate situations when there are lives at stake, there is always someone trying to take advantage!

I thought about how I could make the vessel steer without a rudder, and so decided to take some of the timber from what is commonly called the birth in the bow. I intended to make some sort of a handle on it and use it as a rudder. I had plenty of tools and I still had a bit of time so, I started to work on it. It seemed to be a good idea and I thought it would work. Then I received another message from a ship. The captain asked me if we had a satellite phone, and if so, he would call me, that way other people would not hear our conversation on the HF radio. He told me he was about five hours away and he thought it was very bad the way the Australian Government was not prepared to help us.

He told me to put out a sea anchor to help hold our position (a sea anchor is like a small parachute that you drag in the water to slow a vessel down). I have to say here that the captain had every intention of supplying any assistance he could, I thought we were going to be rescued but it was just the beginning of more dramas, ending with the total destruction of our yacht!

We were drifting with a south westerly current at around four knots, we were by now only about twenty-four hours from the Great Barrier Reef. The captain of the freighter asked me to raise a radar reflector which we already had up, (a radar reflector lets other vessels see you more clearly on their radar screen). He said he'd be there in about four hours. At that stage I wasn't sure what his plan was, but we were just glad that someone was prepared to render assistance.

The weather was fine and sunny, but there was still a large

swell running. With the sails down the yacht was bobbing around like a cork in the sea. The depth of the sea was about four thousand metres, with the sea anchor out we were drifting very slowly. The water was so clear that we could see the sea anchor quite easily at a depth of seventy metres. Two beautiful rainbow-coloured fish of about a meter long, swam fearlessly around the boat with innocent curiosity. It was such a nice moment in such a dangerous situation.

Some four hours after our previous radio communication with the ship, a spec began to grow on the horizon. An hour or so later the container ship stood off by about half a mile. The captain sent a dinghy over to us with a mechanic to see if he could fix our steering. The mechanic and his offsider climbed down into our engine room, but the yacht was rolling so much that they soon became chronically seasick and were forced to return to the ship. I went with them to speak to the captain and explained they were unable to fix our steering. I suggested a tow, but he said that was out of the question, as the yacht would not tow straight, and would turn and probably capsize or breakup. Instead, he suggested to load the yacht onto the ship! He spoke with such confidence I assumed he'd done it before. I couldn't believe my ears and asked him sincerely, "Are you telling me you can load the yacht onto this ship?"

"Yes," he said, he told me that he would use one of the cranes on board; I thought to myself, 'This is fantastic, all our problems are solved.'

It was about four o'clock in the afternoon, with the ships dinghy's assistance, the yacht was brought alongside the ship. The plan was to then put two straps under the yacht and attach them to the hook of the crane. This was similar to the way a travel lift picks a yacht up for slipping, the only difference is that a travel lift would have a spreader bar.

Eventually two large straps were placed around the hull of the yacht, then all that had to be done was to catch the swinging hook from the crane. To cut a long story short, the ship's crew men were running in all directions trying to secure/catch the 'hook.'

It appeared quite chaotic to me standing on the upper deck of the big ship. Every time the ship rolled — the uncontrolled swinging hook from the crane, would strike something on our boat as it swung past breaking it completely off, and slinging it into the sea! First it struck one of the spreaders snapping it off like a carrot. On its return swing it ripped off our new radar sending it flying into the sea. On its third swing it took out another one of the spreaders, then returned to tear a gaping hole in our brand-new headsail! This continued until there was just the mast sticking up from the yacht, held on by only a few remaining stays.

After about an hour of almost total destruction to our topsides, the crane hook was finally caught by the crew, and shackled to the straps making it possible for the crane to take the load and lift the yacht out of the water. Once the yacht had been lifted clear of the water, it started to swing uncontrollably. Each time the ship rolled, the yacht being lighter in weight would not swing at the same time and would crash instead onto the side of the steel ship. Eventually the gunwales got crushed, a huge hole the size of a man's head was punched right through the starboard side, fortunately above the waterline.

This smashing and crashing continued until what was left of our yacht was finally lifted above the side of the ship. After many hours the boat was hauled on deck and placed between four containers — on four thin coconut mats!

I didn't know much about containers at the time but on the top of each container is a square locating block which is designed for stacking purposes. When one container is placed on top of another, it won't slide off. The driver of the crane was only used to handling these steel containers, and was very rough. He dropped the yacht the last half meter or so onto a position between two stacks of containers.

My wife and I were on the bridge of the ship watching what was left of our once beautiful yacht being loaded. When it hit the containers, we both heard a loud crack! I thought then that no doubt more damage had just occurred. I didn't know then that the yacht was resting its twenty-six tons on four small sharp blocks of steel, needless to say when the crane driver dropped our yacht the last half meter it punched four holes straight into the hull of the yacht.

When we asked the captain's first mate if we could go and inspect the yacht for any hull damage, we were told we were not allowed to go out on the deck. The captain told us that the next stop was Port Moresby in Papua New Guinea. He assured us that when we arrived, repairs could be made at the local yacht club where we would then be able to continue with our voyage. We were given a small medical cabin with a rock-hard bed — but were grateful for it anyway, we soon fell asleep.

On arrival in Port Moresby the ship was berthed, Papua New Guinean customs came aboard to check all our passports. Although none of us had visas, they were helpful and issued temporary visas for us given our circumstances.

It was about ten o'clock at night before unloading began. The captain told me the yacht would be off loaded first. The ship was tied up on the port side where all the containers were to be stacked; that meant our yacht would be off loaded into the water on the starboard side. It would be left there until all the containers were off loaded the following morning. It would then be towed to the marina for repairs. We were asked to stay in our cabin and basically keep out of the way, so we tried to catch up on some rest although the adrenaline was still well and truly up.

At about eleven-fifteen p.m. the engineer came knocking on the door and asked me hurriedly, "Where are your bilge pumps located?" I said to him, "Why, what's wrong?" He replied, "Your yacht is taking in water and sinking." I couldn't believe my ears. I told him the bilge pumps wouldn't work because the engine had failed. "What a silly man," I thought.

I then asked, "What about your ship's bilge pumps?" He immediately ordered a crew member to go and retrieve one of their ship's bilge pumps.

In the meantime, we had made our way down to the yacht. I couldn't believe my eyes, the only thing that was stopping the yacht from sinking in the Port Moresby harbour were the two straps that were still around the hull and attached to the crane head. The yacht was submerged to the top of the deck! The only thing above the water was part of the cockpit cabin and the mast. The crane seemed able to hold the yacht in position, but was unable to lift it because it was now full of water — it was far too heavy!

I jumped onto the yacht and quickly tried to unplug the few remaining electronics that were still above water, I passed them to my wife who was standing above me on the ship. I screamed out at the engineer saying, "Why did it sink?" But of course, nobody appeared to know, or rather didn't want to say. I knew then that this was the end of our trip.

The ship had two cranes on board, one was in use holding

the yacht from sinking into Port Moresby harbour, while the other crane proceeded to unload the containers onto the other side of the vessel. Eventually at about three a.m., the bilge pump arrived from the engineer's workshop, as it also had broken down! They finally got it going and slowly the water in our yacht started to recede. As it receded, the yacht became lighter, eventually the crane was able to lift her out of the water. The yacht was craned right across the top of the ship with water streaming out from the four holes in the hull!

I knew immediately that the holes in the boat had been caused by the crane operator when he dropped our yacht. What a terrible sight it was; everything on the yacht was destroyed, even the few electronics I had tried to save ended up destroyed with salt water damage. The only thing we had left were the clothes we were wearing. The next day we were allowed to inspect what was left of our yacht. One of our new freezers was full of fresh fish which we gave to the locals, all the rest of the food was destroyed; there had been enough food on board for six months.

We stayed one night in Port Moresby at some type of compound, the next day my wife and I flew back to Brisbane. The other two crew members hitched a ride on a freighter going north, we never heard from them again!

I was very annoyed with them as apparently, they had inspected the yacht before she was unloaded, they knew about the holes in the hull from fraternising and drinking with the ship's crew, but they had chosen not to tell us, why? One can only guess… Had they told me, I could have patched the holes up with a quick repair kit on board. A temporary patch could have enabled the boat to be taken to the slip for more permanent repairs, and so would have saved our yacht.

On arrival in Brisbane, we had nowhere to stay and very little money, we bought a tent and erected it in a caravan park. We stayed there for six months. During that period, it rained and rained.

It was Christmas, we knew nobody other than the girl next door who lived in a tent permanently, she had bigger problems but was kind enough to invite us in on Xmas day to share her humble tent and TV. You soon get to know who cares when you're in a situation like that. In the meantime, the shipping company that had destroyed our yacht, offered to bring it back to Brisbane when they were next in Port Moresby.

When it finally arrived, we were devastated to see how the once pristine yacht was now almost totally destroyed. There she sat at Fisherman's Wharf in Brisbane, the hull propped up by steel acro-props and the mast laying alongside with a heap of tangled rigging still partly attached. To add insult to injury, the authorities at the wharf told us the yacht had to be moved within three days, after which they were going to charge us a six hundred dollar-a-day penalty.

We frantically tried to find a yard close by where we could store the yacht to start repairs. There was only one yard nearby and fortunately for us they had room, so we arranged for a semi-trailer to take the yacht to the yard. The following day a logistics company with the assistance of a crane at the wharf, turned up at the yard with our yacht. We had hired a crane to offload the yacht at the yard. Another semi-trailer had to be hired just to bring what was left of the mast down to the yard. The crane hire, and the two semi-trailers with a police escort, cost us another ten thousand dollars.

Looking back, I wish I had fixed the emergency steering and continued on back to Australia ourselves. So there we were, with our yacht that we had worked so hard on for thirteen years, now stuck in a yard in Brisbane in a totally wrecked state!

At the boat yard, the yacht was placed on steel poles and a borrowed ladder was used to enable us to climb aboard.

It hit us hard when we realised how much damage had been done by the saltwater and the boat being in the tropics for six months. A lot of the food still lay rotting in the bilges and cupboards, stale salt water lay in pools around it; we had a job in front of us to say the least.

It took us six more months of hard work and another fifty thousand dollars we borrowed to get the yacht back into a good enough state to sell. When we did sell her, the best price we could get was fifty thousand dollars, so the whole exercise had been for nothing!

The day we sold it, we drove out of the yard, I said to my wife, "Don't look back." But that wasn't the end of it.

We had purchased a very cheap wooden catamaran to live on while the sale went through. I had obtained a mooring in the Brisbane River, so we at least had somewhere to stay, live and sleep.

One morning while standing in the cockpit of our old catamaran having a cup of coffee. I was looking down the river when I saw the bow of a vessel I recognised, as it grew larger. I could see it was our old boat! I couldn't believe my eyes, I called out to my wife to quickly come, I said, "Look here comes the old boat." We both just stood there not talking, just looking as we saw her being tied to a couple of old mooring posts. The man we had sold it to tied her up, then locking her up we saw him get off the boat, he was then driven away by somebody in a car. We both just shook our heads wondering what next, was this boat haunting us?

For the next three years the old boat stayed tied up to the

wooden posts, by then we had sold our catamaran and moved on.

I remember hearing about the massive Brisbane floods, apparently the old boat that we spent thirteen years doing up had broken its lines and washed out to sea never to be seen again.

I keep thinking about that little voice that had said to me, "Don't do it."

It took me thirteen years to see the brick wall! I was definitely not on the right track as interesting as it was.

Just imagine what the other track might have been like.

"I JUST DIDN'T TAKE ANY NOTICE!"

Chapter 28

A Profit, Just in Time

During the restoration of the yacht, before we started our overseas world trip, we had been admiring our old house in Bundaberg that we had lovingly restored. We used to drive-by to see how the garden was growing etc.

One day I was driving by and saw a for sale sign on the house. I immediately went to the agent to see how much the owners wanted for it. To my delight I discovered that real estate values had dropped considerably, hence it was now for sale at a great deal less than what we had sold it for.

Anyway, to cut a long story short, I made an offer that was within a thousand or two of the original price I had purchased it for, before our original restoration! It probably sounds a bit rude, but the real estate market had collapsed and the house was in need of a complete restoration again.

To my amazement my offer was accepted. I quickly made arrangements and borrowed some money again, using our old home in Victoria as collateral — the deal was done.

Because I knew what needed doing to the house, in no time it was completed. We re-carpeted, fixed some broken windows, quickly painted the outside, and re-polished the floors inside. We fixed up the garden, then went down to the agent to get some tenants. We'd had the house about a year, in which time the real estate market improved dramatically.

After losing most of our money with the yacht catastrophe, I was looking for any way I could to recuperate some funds. So I called the agent and asked what he thought about selling. He was Greek and had been very good to us with getting the right tenants and generally looking after things. I asked him, "What do you thinks it's worth?" He said to me with a strong Greek accent, "Geoff, I get you a hundred and fifty thousand, no problem."

"Are you serious?" I asked.

"Yes," he replied, "No problem."

"Okay," I replied, "Anything over a hundred and fifty thousand is yours."

Two weeks later he called me and said, "It's sold Geoff, and I have the hundred and fifty for you."

I don't know to this day how much he got, but I was happy to recoup some of the lost funds and I think he was happy also.

"KEEP YOUR CHIN UP — THINGS ARE NEVER AS BAD AS THEY SEEM."

Chapter 29

The Poodles

My wife and I were returning from an overseas trip. The year was 2009 and we'd left our two poodles, Max and Goldie with my wife's aunt, she was to look after them while we were away. On our return they went crazy as they were so excited to see us.

Once they had settled down, I decided to go to the shop to get some food. I took the poodles in the car as I was sure that they would not let me go without them this time.

It was a warm day and I decided to leave the windows down in the car so they wouldn't get too hot while I was in the supermarket. I was shopping for about half an hour, and wasn't concerned about the dogs as we had done this many times previously.

When I came back to the car with my shopping trolley, I found there was only one dog! The other one had jumped out apparently. I loaded the shopping into the car and immediately started looking for Goldie, but she was nowhere to be seen. I searched the car park high and low, after about two hours, I realised she must have gone further afield. It was very unlike her, normally she never left the car, but it seemed likely she had panicked thinking I was leaving without her again.

I drove around the whole area for several hours looking for her. I asked everybody I saw on the road had they seen a small white poodle, but nobody had seen her. It was getting late and becoming too dark to continue searching, I knew it was pointless going on looking for her. So I went back home and did the usual phoning around. I called all the local vets, the dog pound, the RSPCA to let them know about my little lost dog Goldie. The next morning I awoke early, and went straight back down to the supermarket to continue my search for her.

I spent many hours that morning searching for her, but there was no sign of Goldie. Eventually after many hours I gave up trying to find her. I parked the car and said to my higher self, "I can't find her, please take me to where she is." I started the car up and just followed the road without thinking. It took me up the hill where I had already driven the day before, I didn't question it even though I was aware I had been there the day before.

This time I went a little further, then for no reason I stopped, as I did so I saw a little lane off to my left. I looked up the lane and then out of the long grass came a very tired and disheveled looking poodle.

At that stage she hadn't even seen me, she was just walking down the lane. I quickly opened the passenger door and called out to her, "Goldie, Goldie, jump in." Although she got in the car straightaway, I don't think she realised it was me, but after a second or two she became very excited and knew she was with her family again. I was so excited — I was cuddling her and holding her and she responded with licks and squeaks.

We went back home and all was well again. Goldie's higher self clearly contacted my higher self-there's no doubt about that.

The important thing about this little story is, it proves there is a higher-self that sees all, and if you ask and let go of your own ideas, you will be guided always.

"YOU WILL BE HELPED."

Chapter 30

The Little Voice

I have been listening to my spiritual voice for a long time now, and it never ceases to amaze me how accurate it is. For example, I often say to my wife, "I'm going to the trash and treasure market to buy certain things we need." I never go down to the market hoping that the thing is maybe there, on the contrary, I go down knowing that they will be there!

I will give you an example. I was building and fitting out a motor home once. I had painted the vehicle a metallic steel grey. I had fitted all the windows and wanted to buy some blinds for them. So I went to the market, and as I walked through, one of the stalls had a bundle of grey blinds. I said to the man, "How much do you want for those?" He replied, "I can't sell them, they're the wrong colour it seems, no one wants grey blinds. I don't want to take them home, so you can have them for five dollars."

I didn't count them, I just bundled them up and took them back to the car, thinking to myself, *well at least they're the right colour*.

When I got home, I unpacked the car and counted the blinds, there was exactly the right number and the right size for a complete fit out of the camper! The best thing was they were only five dollars!

This type of thing has happened to me on so many

occasions... I just listen, focus in, and then put it aside and don't worry, I just let it happen.

I have bought numerous things of considerable value this way... Once I bought a yacht worth over two hundred thousand dollars in Thailand, sight unseen! People say to me, "How can you do that? Aren't you worried that it may not be right?" This is exactly the point I am trying to make, doubt creates worry and concern, when those two things come into play, well that's the end of it for you. You have to trust a hundred percent, have no doubt whatsoever, and then it will start to work. I will take it further than that, you have to know it. Hoping it will be right is not sufficient — know it.

"TRUST IN THE NATURAL SYSTEM."

Chapter 31

Susanna

My wife and I ran a bed and breakfast for many years in the Dandenong Ranges. It was quite successful and after some time we needed a holiday. We decided to employ a manageress named Susanna. She was a single parent and had a young daughter of about eleven years old.

We thought this situation would suit her well as there would be no rent to pay, only light duties, it was also somewhere nice for her and her daughter to live.

I arranged with the bank to give her a credit card with a maximum of five hundred dollars withdrawal, that way she always had funds for shopping etc. for the guests.

Confidently we headed up north to Sydney, towing a caravan. On arrival in Sydney, we were having dinner at my brother's home, when after speaking with Susanna on the phone, I suddenly got a strong feeling I should return to Melbourne immediately as I somehow knew that there was something very wrong.

My wife asked what was going on, so I told her, "I don't know, we just have to go back home straight away." She started preparing for the trip back in the caravan but again I said, "Oh no, we haven't got time to tow the caravan, we have to drive immediately and quickly." She was used to this sort of thing happening. So we headed off driving all night, leaving the caravan at my brother's place in Sydney.

Arriving twelve hours later at our little village in the Dandenongs, I said to my wife, "We should buy a little food before we drive to the bed and breakfast," which was only a hundred meters away.

As we parked the car and prepared to walk into the shop, I saw Susanna, the woman we had employed. I said to her, "What are you doing here?" It was about eight a.m., breakfast time at the B&B. She said, "I'm finished," and walked away, I was very annoyed but didn't have time to question her on why she was going, I just needed to get back home to the unaware customers.

I didn't know what was going on — when we arrived at the bed and breakfast ten minutes later, the house was full of guests. Some were taking showers, some were still in bed, but most still hadn't paid, and none had had their breakfast. Susanna had just walked out and left a mess. Luckily, I had listened to my intuition, and returned immediately otherwise just imagine what would've happened.

We got everything straightened out, but had to forfeit our holiday; in fact, I had to go back to Sydney to pick up the caravan. I asked Susanna later what had happened. She just said it was all too much.

I went to the bank and cancelled her credit card the day after she left, so she would have no access to our account. Telephone banking was new then, about six months after Susanna had left, she got her telephone banking set up, when she discovered she was still linked to our account.

On January 3rd I noticed that there was less money in our account than there should have been. I decided to get a copy of the bank statement to see what was going on, and discovered due to an error at the bank, Susanna was now robbing our account systematically, and had been doing so for a couple of months. When my account had a few thousand dollars in it, she would transfer six or seven hundred dollars. If the account had say, eleven or twelve hundred dollars in it, she would only transfer two or three hundred dollars. I went to the bank and complained bitterly. They immediately rectified the issue and repaid us all money that was taken and consequently Susanna was arrested.

This is just another little story about taking notice of your higher self.

"LISTEN AND FOLLOW YOUR GIVEN DIRECTIONS"

Chapter 32

The Producer

Years ago, I carved onto an old piece of driftwood the words: 'LISTEN TO YOURSELF, FOR YOU ARE YOUR OWN GUIDE.' I gave it to my daughter who was fifteen at the time. She's now married with three children and still treasures it.

That little voice you hear is yourself, or rather your higher self as I like to call it. By reading this book about some of the odd and strange things that happened in my life, I hope you will come to an understanding about life as I have; knowing that it is forever, and that our existence here is just like a play. In the play we have a role and when our part is over, we get to meet the producer!

In the spirit world there is no beginning or end, so time as we know it, doesn't exist there. This means from our point of view every choice in life that is possible, or has been possible, or will be possible, is already written in, the great book of life!

Einstein discovered that time can be bent! Not being a scientist, I'm not going to get into that too much.

I would like to tell you a short story here about what happened to me regarding time. In the 1970's, I was in a pretty bad car accident. It was a head-on collision with another vehicle, and although I don't remember all the details of the accident, I do remember the impact and the steering column coming towards my head.

The car I was driving was built in the late-50s and didn't have a collapsible steering column like the cars have today. As the steering column came towards my head, I remember trying to move away from it... The strange thing was that the steering column was moving quite slowly, all my attempts to move away from it were also quite slow — in the end I was unable to move away in time. My point here is that something happened with time at that moment, either 'things' slowed down, or my mind sped up. In a sense, time is able to move around and alters slightly every moment, back and forth.

For a child waiting for the next Christmas to come, it seems like an eternity, yet for an older person it seems to come around too quickly.

When you're on holidays and having a great time, your holiday seems to end too soon, whereas for a prisoner in solitary confinement, they start to go crazy in a few days. Time is just a perception of our understanding, and is variable.

Take a butterfly for example, it lives for three days but enjoys a full life. Don't forget time is only our way of dividing the distance between a beginning and an end in a material world.

I was climbing a ladder one day that apparently wasn't quite level, it slipped and I fell to the ground. I remember falling very slowly with the ladder, in fact I even had time to contemplate how long it was going to take before I hit the ground. The distance I fell was only about two meters, so it happened very fast — or did it? What exactly happened? I have no idea, but time definitely moved around somehow.

Anyhow, putting that aside, time only exists in the physical realm we all exist in, but the spirit/soul never dies. The physical life we experience here is barely a sliver of the real existence. We are limited here by our five physical senses, plus our lack of knowledge and understanding.

The advice on which direction to take in life is usually gleaned from our parents, or guardians, and our upbringing in general. Intuition does not play much of a part in it, but it should. It should be part of the curriculum in my opinion, to teach children about the power of the spirit and what is really going on. All we are ever taught is what's going on in the material world. It's almost as though there is no spiritual world. How naive is that?

Our soul is the body's driver or helmsman, and without it the body would just drop to the ground, so it makes sense to learn about the driver and what it is capable of. The soul is our driver and our guide; we should be listening and acting on what it says all the time — remember that little voice.

Life is like a book, it has already been written, and that is proved by the fact that some people can see into what we call the future. All they are really doing is skipping a few pages in 'the book', and having a look ahead at possibilities or probabilities in the following chapters.

In saying that life is all about choices. We make our own path as we travel along this journey. There is no right or wrong path, there is just a multitude of choices, and therefore a multitude of outcomes/consequences. It's all about experiences. We arrive here and play our small part in this incredible book, going from page to page — chapter to chapter, and year after year. As we progress, our physical bodies get older and older. We call this a passage of time, or a life. Don't forget this book of choices has already been written and all we are doing is acting out our version of it, which is determined by the decisions we make whether they be logical or intuitive.

The logical way makes more immediate sense to most, and

it sometimes seems easier to follow, but it is not the best way to live an interesting life of experiences and surprises.

The intuitive way (not to be confused with being a fatalist) is more testing, because some of the time the decisions we make don't make sense at that moment, and are impossible to justify. Because we can't see the outcome like the spirit can, we plod along on the left brain's logical track. If we knew what was around the corner, we probably wouldn't do half the things we do.

If you want to develop your connection with the spirit or soul, then it's only a matter of listening, trusting and acting. It's all about trust. If you trust in the natural intuitive system, then life becomes easier and much more interesting with many good outcomes.

When we meet somebody for the first time, we sometimes get a feeling that we already know that person, and sometimes they may feel the same way. Yet we are both sure we have never met before. I believe that these two people do actually know each other, the souls have recognised each other from the spirit world — the real world. Some people call this chemistry, and to be fair part of it is chemistry because the two physical bodies understand there is a connection. Other people use the term soulmate which is also correct.

When we meet someone that we feel we know or have known, there is recognition of some sort that passes between the two souls that is converted to a feeling the two bodies understand. Many people call this feeling chemistry. Imagine two people that already know each other quite well, and unbeknown to each other, they both go to the same fancy-dress party. They bump into each other at the party not realising they would both be there. At first they don't recognise each other through their physical eyes because of their costumes, but they soon realise that there is something familiar, so then they may ask, "Don't I know you from somewhere?" or perhaps, "Haven't we met before?" When two souls meet that know each other, the feeling is converted to the physical body, but at a fancy-dress party our doubt leaves us unsure.

When you get to know somebody well, you tend to look past their physical appearance and see in your mind's eye the real person, or the soul. This proves that we are spiritual beings only wearing a costume i.e., the physical body.

In Australia sometimes when it's really hot, I go to the cinema to see a movie and to enjoy the air-conditioned comfort. It's often just an excuse to catch up on a movie that I had missed, but after sitting in air-conditioned comfort watching a gripping movie that maybe set in a colder climate, I'm often quite surprised when I go outside again to find it is still hot and sunny! It's a very different place.

Life here in the physical is very much like that, we arrive and act out our part in the play, and when the play is over, we leave and go back to our real world, the spirit world. The fact that we have to arrive (birth) and leave (death) to act here in this life/play, tells me that it is temporary, as such it cannot possibly be the main or real part of our existence. This play is so well constructed, we feel it is real, and in a sense, things are real in the play.

Imagine for a moment we were one of the characters in the movie, and the movie would be our only world. The movie would have to be running all the time for us to exist indefinitely, but it isn't — it has a beginning and an end, therefore proving that this is not our real world, but just a temporary place we visit to experience 'situations'.

The driver or the soul never dies, the soul is absolutely

necessary to operate the body and make it move. The soul and our physical body work very closely together, intermingling in harmony, a bit like a hand and a glove. The glove, representing the body is useless until the hand, representing the soul, enters it, then it becomes alive. When the hand is taken out from the glove, it becomes useless again, we call that death, when in fact it is just the spirit returning home.

As the body needs food and rest to recover from work, so the spirit also needs to be reconnected to its home to replenish its energy source to be able to continue working together in harmony. Hence the two do this at the same time. We call it sleep, it is absolutely essential to both the spirit and the body of all creatures, as every creature has a soul, which is part of the spirit world.

We need to remind ourselves that while we have individual bodies here, we are ONE in the real world, and therefore every time we hurt, degrade, or even kill, we are doing it to ourselves! We have to stop thinking as individuals and remember that we are all part of the ONE in absolute reality.

The spirit world, where everything is forever, is our true home. In the spirit world there is no time, as time only effects things with a beginning and an end making the spirit world a place that is always, and always is.

Imagine if you were to cut up a book and lay the pages out one after the other. First of all, there would be a beginning and an end, there would also be a distance between the first page and the last page. It would take time to read the pages, that's why we think everything is attached to this thing we call time, when in fact time is simply a tool to measure a distance from a beginning to an end. This then gives us understanding of how this play, called life, is set up here.

Now imagine the spirit world where all the pages of this incredible book are not flowing one after the other, but are stacked on top of each other. Also imagine that they are transparent so you can look into all or any of the pages of the big story at the same time. You would be able to see it all.

That's what I mean about there being no time in the spirit world, because everything just IS RIGHT NOW.

Try looking at it in the following scenario, imagine a wave in the ocean. Now consider that what is behind the wave or following the wave is the past, the crest of the wave is now, and the rest of the wave that appears to be pushed along in front is the future. My point is, the only thing that's really happening is what is happening now. The water that's following the wave is the past and therefore is only a memory that does not exist anymore. The water in front of the wave being pushed along, is only a possibility and does not exist as it hasn't happened yet from our perspective. The only thing that really is happening is on the crest of the wave which is right now...

We enter the great book at some stage or chapter, we act out our version as we go along. The play is written, but we make up the words and our own lines as we go. There are endless opportunities throughout this journey. The whole procedure is called life and it's fantastic! Life can be very stimulating and exciting, if we allow ourselves to follow our own personal guidance. If you listen, you will realise it is trying to talk to us all the time. We call the little voice we hear in our heads by many different names. Some people call it intuition, others guidance from above or guidance from our higher self, or even God. I think it is the spiritual side of ourselves we hear... that is, our own spirit talking to us and advising us, because it sees all, as in the physical world we are restricted. If we knew what was going to happen, what would be the point of the play?

Obviously, these messages do not come in a loud verbal voice but in the form of thoughts and feelings and often symbols. Many people find it difficult to tell the difference between the spiritual guidance thoughts, and the regular logical thoughts from the left brain. The more you listen and respond to your personal guide, the more messages you receive. After a while you learn to tell the difference between spiritual advice and logical thinking, it just comes naturally, because it is the natural and the correct way. It doesn't really matter what you like to call it, it's all the same. It's the little voice that is always trying to help you.

One of the reasons we often take no notice of it is because we are not taught. There are two sides to our brain, the left side is the logical side, and the right side is the intuitive side. The conflict begins when a thought comes to us, we either act on it (right brain) or we start to analyse it (left brain). The latter immediately creates doubts, and when you have doubts, it's usually the end of the unpolluted thought. We then start analysing the pros and cons and start to modify the thought. It isn't long before the thought has changed altogether, and we now have a new thought from the left logical brain! It may or may not work out, but you have just missed the best advice, and no doubt a better track, but you'll never know!

There are many ways to go on our journey through life, many different roads that we can travel on, which is exactly the way it is meant to be. We are almost totally influenced and controlled by the way society is set up, i.e., education, the need to seek the best job, bringing up children with the so called 'right' beliefs, having a certain type of house in the best suburb, or driving the latest car etc. All these pressures are dictated to us as being the 'correct' way to go, and they seem logical. We almost always follow the logical way because it seems correct, right? What's really happening is we become predictable, as in a football game... If we know which way the player is going to turn and run with that precious ball he's holding, then he is easy to tackle. Business people and governments all take advantage of this 'weakness', yes, I say weakness because we don't trust in ourselves, and as a result we become very easily manipulated. Then the big boys throw in a little fear, which is then whipped up by the media, and in no time they have us jumping through hoops. The only way these business people and governments can control us so easily, is because we invariably take the logical way and become very predictable and therefore easy to control.

We are all in this trap to one degree or another. When I realised what was going on with my right and left brain, I decided to try my hardest to use my right brain for most of the decisions I make, it's working well! Don't forget governments and big businesses cannot survive without us, the fact is, the only reason governments and big business have so much power over us, is because we have become so predictable. I'm not saying here that we don't need businesses, we do need them because of the way this society is set up, but I intensely dislike the control and manipulation that big business and governments wield over us. They need us to survive therefore we should, and must, control them.

The so-called rules or laws they design are meant to keep us working, and therefore under their control. They don't allow us to have any time for ourselves to mature spiritually, in fact, in some countries, spiritualism is discouraged, why? The system has gone full circle, the very governments that we voted in to work for us, now have us working for them!

Remember, we are only caretakers while we are here, we do

not own anything, but it is worth being reminded that everything we think we own, will sooner or later be taken from us. Even if it's just when we leave the play. We place far too much value on our material possessions, and at the same time we place very little value on our spiritual development.

Some people would practically sell their soul for material gain, while spiritually they are in reverse gear! We should constantly remind ourselves that this is only a play, and when we leave the stage, we leave everything behind. All these so-called possessions we foolishly think we own, are in fact only 'props' for the play. We should enjoy the ride and not be too materialistic or emotionally affected by the other actors in the play.

We are trained/indoctrinated from the word go. Children watch cartoons on TV most of which are violent to one degree or another, on top of all that, there is religious indoctrination which does nothing but segregate the population.

How childish it is for people to argue between each other about what their God may have said e.g., my God said this, or my God said that. It's gone so far that people are prepared to kill each other over some petty argument. It's the type of argument you would expect to hear from five-year-old school children in the school playground.

Wouldn't it be fantastic if all people took the intuitive track in life, governments, big business and religion would be unable to control and manipulate us? We would be unpredictable and life would be so different and so much better.

The window to gaining knowledge is there for everybody. Some people get the message in dreams, others get what they call premonitions, but it's all the same. The most important thing is to act on your personal message. If you don't, you will probably find yourself on the wrong track. Not acting/responding to what you hear is the same as denying you have a spirit. You are also closing the door to any more messages. The more you respond to your personal messages, the more often the door opens for you, and the better life will be for you.

I am sure we have all noticed sometimes we get a strong feeling of perhaps caution or fear, or maybe that you feel you know the person. These feelings are sensors your soul picks up to alert you via your physical body.

Imagine for a moment that the whole of the Earth is surrounded by an imaginary bubble that constantly changes shape and size depending on certain conditions. It extends everywhere around the planet and is full of energy created by the life force of humans, animals, and flora. Humans are very powerful, especially when collectively thinking. They can create and do create change. In fact, the human race is a product of its collective thinking, so there is no need to blame anybody other than ourselves for the way things are. Things are what they are because of our collectively thinking, which means they won't change until we collectively decide to change them.

It's all down to us as a collective... We have the power necessary to change things. We can think negatively about each other, and if the thought is strong enough, we create war, as is happening right now. We can change this by thinking positively. Depending on the number of people collectively thinking about the same thing at the same time, we can change things straight away so let's do it!

I found this article on the internet, it shows what can be done collectively. A carefully controlled scientific demonstration of collective thinking and meditation was carried out between June 7 & July 30, 1993. The study involved groups, who increased in number from eight hundred to a maximum of four thousand, over the trial. A week or so after the start of the study, violent crime homicides, rapes and aggravated assaults measured by FBI began decreasing, and continued to drop until the end of the experiment.

Before the project, the researchers had publicly predicted that the group would reduce crime by twenty percent. This prediction had been ridiculed by the Chief of Police, who asserted that the only thing that would decrease crime that much would be twenty inches of snow. In the end, the maximum decrease was twenty-three-point three percent. This significant reduction occurred when the size of the group was at its largest in the final week of the project, and during a blistering heat wave! After the trial stopped, crime again started to rise again.

This is proof that collective thinking can and does affect an outcome!

Years ago, I decided to start a business in Cairns in the tourist industry. I was building a horse drawn wagon to be used to take tourists around the inner city. Unknown to me at the same time, another person was building a wagon in Manly, Sydney, at the same time. We both opened our businesses at almost the same time, within two weeks of each other. One of us, or both of us, had picked up the idea unintentionally from the bubble. This meant that both of us had been working on a similar project for about a year. This is often why people think of an idea, perhaps to go into business, then someone else does exactly the same thing in a completely different part of the country.

When an idea comes to you, you can be sure that if you don't act on it someone else will. This is what I mean when I talk about the invisible bubble around the planet… there are also smaller bubbles, fields around countries, and smaller ones around cities, and if you go really small, there are fields around individual humans and animals.

You have probably all had this experience when someone is introduced to you for the first time, you pick up a sense at the time of the introduction. The closer you get to the person the stronger the feeling is, this is because in a sense you are entering into the bubble that surrounds them, and likewise they are entering into yours. Some of these bubbles that people have around them are so big that you can sense them the instant they walk into a room. These people with exceptionally big bubbles, can sometimes be important people but mostly they only think they are, and just have a big 'ego'. That's okay if you like the person, you can feel at ease and comfortable in that situation. On the other side of the coin, you sometimes meet a person and the closer you get, the more uncomfortable you feel. This is a two-way street by the way, as they can, depending on how sensitive they are, feel uncomfortable as well. A sign to be wary! It is a warning, and if you don't heed it, you can easily end up on the wrong track again.

For example, one day we were having a BBQ, it was a sunny day and most of the guests had already arrived, but one couple were late. I'd started the cooking, suddenly I felt exhausted, I knew that the late guests were very near because I was picking up a woman's severe depression she often suffered with. Sure enough, about five minutes later they walked in all smiles, for me there was no hiding how she was feeling inside.

I know you all have probably had this feeling that I'm talking about at one time or another, but often we are in a situation where we have to push on anyhow, it may be simply a work situation for example, but as I said, the spirit or our personal guide, is always trying to help us, even if we aren't listening most of the time.

"LISTEN TO YOURSELF FOR YOU ARE YOUR OWN

GUIDE."

My Life Today.

Today my wife and I live in Tasmania on fifty acres in the beautiful Huon Valley overlooking the Huon River. I probably would not have written this book had it not been for my wife's encouragement, she is a wonderful wife and companion and we are great friends. My thanks to her.

One of the reasons we moved to the Huon valley was to be in an area that was totally unaffected by artificial or human energies. I feel we found the right place. Our home is totally self-sufficient; all our power and hot water is solar generated, we collect our rainwater, our heating is hydronic, and we have an enviro cycle sanitary system.

These are the things that work for me spiritually:

1. Remember that this existence is only a play and temporary.
2. Allow yourself a period of time each day for self-development, this does not necessarily mean sitting and meditating, although meditation can be quite helpful.
3. The door to your spiritual contact opens every time you have an altered state of mind.

What is an altered state of mind? An altered state of mind is when you just start staring into thin air... Sometimes I find that it is almost like a magnet and can become mesmerising. On other occasions, when your door is open a little, is just before you go to sleep — or just before you are fully awake. At those moments your door is open and thoughts, ideas and contact with your higher self can and does happen.

4. Sometimes just doing mundane and repetitious jobs where you don't have to think can also lead to your door opening. There is no need to work at it, animals do it naturally, just take a look at any cat! Remember don't place too much emphasis on material things, because when your part in the play is over, you walk off the stage empty-handed with nothing but the wisdom you have gleaned.

"STAY AT PEACE WITH THE WORLD."